Pestalozzi and the Educationalization of the World

Other Palgrave Pivot titles

Geraldine Vaughan: The 'Local' Irish in the West of Scotland, 1851–1921

Matthew Feldman: Ezra Pound's Fascist Propaganda, 1935–45

Albert N. Link and John T. Scott: Bending the Arc of Innovation: Public Support of R&D in Small, Entrepreneurial Firms

Amir Idris: Identity, Citizenship, and Violence in Two Sudans: Reimagining a Common Future

G. Douglas Atkins: T.S. Eliot and the Failure to Connect: Satire and Modern Misunderstandings

Piero Formica: Stories of Innovation for the Millennial Generation: The Lynceus Long View

J. David Alvis and Jason R. Jividen: Statesmanship and Progressive Reform: An Assessment of Herbert Croly's Abraham Lincoln

David Munro: A Guide to SME Financing

Claudio Giachetti: Competitive Dynamics in the Mobile Phone Industry

R. Mark Isaac and Douglas A. Norton: Just the Facts Ma'am: A Case Study of the Reversal of Corruption in the Los Angeles Police Department

Huw Macartney: The Debt Crisis and European Democratic Legitimacy

Chiara Mio: Towards a Sustainable University: The Ca' Foscari Experience

Jordi Cat: Maxwell, Sutton and the Birth of Color Photography: A Binocular Study

Nevenko Bartulin: Honorary Aryans: National–Racial Identity and Protected Jews in the Independent State of Croatia

Coreen Davis: State Terrorism and Post-transitional Justice in Argentina: An Analysis of Mega Cause I Trial

Deborah Lupton: The Social Worlds of the Unborn

Shelly McKeown: Identity, Segregation and Peace-Building in Northern Ireland: A Social Psychological Perspective

Rita Sakr: 'Anticipating' the 2011 Arab Uprisings: Revolutionary Literatures and Political Geographies

Timothy Jenkins: Of Flying Saucers and Social Scientists: A Re-Reading of When Prophecy Fails and of Cognitive Dissonance

Ben Railton: The Chinese Exclusion Act: What It Can Teach Us about America

Patrick Joseph Ryan: Master-Servant Childhood: A History of the Idea of Childhood in Medieval English Culture

Andrew Dowdle, Scott Limbocker, Song Yang, Karen Sebold, and Patrick A. Stewart: Invisible Hands of Political Parties in Presidential Elections: Party Activists and Political Aggregation from 2004 to 2012

Jean-Paul Gagnon: Evolutionary Basic Democracy: A Critical Overture

Mark Casson and Catherine Casson: The Entrepreneur in History: From Medieval Merchant to Modern Business Leader

Tracy Shilcutt: Infantry Combat Medics in Europe, 1944–45

Asoka Bandarage: Sustainability and Well-Being: The Middle Path to Environment, Society, and the Economy

palgrave▸pivot

Pestalozzi and the Educationalization of the World

Daniel Tröhler
University of Luxembourg

DOI: 10.1057/9781137346858

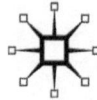

PESTALOZZI AND THE EDUCATIONALIZATION OF THE WORLD
Copyright © Daniel Tröhler, 2013.

All rights reserved.

First published in 2013 by
PALGRAVE MACMILLAN®
in the United States—a division of St. Martin's Press LLC,
175 Fifth Avenue, New York, NY 10010.

Where this book is distributed in the UK, Europe and the rest of the world, this is by Palgrave Macmillan, a division of Macmillan Publishers Limited, registered in England, company number 785998, of Houndmills, Basingstoke, Hampshire RG21 6XS.

Palgrave Macmillan is the global academic imprint of the above companies and has companies and representatives throughout the world.

Palgrave® and Macmillan® are registered trademarks in the United States, the United Kingdom, Europe and other countries.

ISBN: 978-1-137-34687-2 EPUB
ISBN: 978-1-137-34685-8 PDF
ISBN: 978-1-137-37182-9 Hardback

Library of Congress Cataloging-in-Publication Data is available from the Library of Congress.

A catalogue record of the book is available from the British Library.

First edition: 2013

www.palgrave.com/pivot

DOI: 10.1057/9781137346858

To my parents, Suzanne and Martin Tröhler-Schweizer, who bought me the voluminous critical edition of the works and letters of Pestalozzi 30 years ago when I was a student.

Contents

Acknowledgments ix

1 The Educationalization of Social Problems Around 1800   1
   1.1 Pestalozzi and the educational turn   2
   1.2 The prehistory of the educational turn   4
   1.3 Commercial progress vs. classical ideal of virtue   7
   1.4 Reformed Protestantism and the educational strengthening of the soul   8

2 Zurich Around 1750: Economic and Cultural Boom and Revolutionary Activities   14
   2.1 The political organization of the Republic of Zurich in the eighteenth century   15
   2.2 Commercialization of societal life in Zurich around 1750   17
   2.3 The fight against corruption and decline   19
   2.4 The republican youth movement in Zurich after 1760   21

3 The Development and Early Fate of a Republican Revolutionary   26
   3.1 Pestalozzi's childhood and youth   27
   3.2 Republican choosing of spouse and occupation   30
   3.3 The classical republic of virtue and the opportunities of early industry—Neuhof   33

3.4	Agriculture with or without early industry?	34

4 The Christian Republic, Enlightenment, and Coercive Education   38
- 4.1 Political reforms and the Christian republic of *Lienhard und Gertrud* (1781)   39
- 4.2 The disillusionment of the Swiss republics   42
- 4.3 The popular Enlightenment and modern natural law   44
- 4.4 *Lienhard und Gertrud*, Parts 3 and 4 (1785 and 1787)   46

5 The American and the French Republics, German Idealism, and the Principle of Inwardness   50
- 5.1 Freedom, property, and social obligations   51
- 5.2 The French Revolution and Pestalozzi's position   54
- 5.3 The political consequences in the mid-1790s   56
- 5.4 Pestalozzi's *Meine Nachforschungen* (1797) on the eve of the Helvetic Revolution   58

6 The Helvetic Republic and the Discovery of "the Method"   62
- 6.1 The Helvetic Republic in 1798 and hopes for reestablishment of the old republic of virtue   64
- 6.2 The experiment in Stans   66
- 6.3 Burgdorf: "The method"   68

7 Propaganda and Institutional Success   73
- 7.1 State propaganda for and institutional successes of "the Pestalozzi method"   74
- 7.2 Period of suffering and redemption   76
- 7.3 Success abroad and the Pestalozzi cult   78
- 7.4 Politics or education?   80

8 European Demands for New Education: Political, National, Private   83
- 8.1 Pestalozzi and the increasing interest in new educational methods   84
- 8.2 Interest on the part of the political powers   85

	8.3	Interest on the part of activists and concerned parents	87
	8.4	Pestalozzi and the rise of a wide educational public	90
9	Pestalozzi's Charisma, a Guarantee of Success and a Problem		95
	9.1	Growth and success	96
	9.2	Internal conflicts and problems	98
	9.3	Fichte's *Addresses to the German Nation* (1808)	100
	9.4	Education policy interest in "the method"	103
10	Public Critique, Restoration, Pestalozzi's Lonesome End, and the Beginning of Modern Mass Education		105
	10.1	Pestalozzi's fight in vain for official recognition in Switzerland	106
	10.2	Troubled years at the institute in Yverdon	109
	10.3	*An die Unschuld, den Ernst und den Edelmut* (1815)	111
	10.4	The new school for the poor	113
11	The Educationalized World and the Internationalization of the Cult of Pestalozzi		117
	11.1	The final collapse of the institute in Yverdon	118
	11.2	The last new beginning and the end at Neuhof	120
	11.3	Death and the start of a cult	123
12	Pestalozzi, or an Ambiguous Legacy in Education		129
	12.1	Modernization and school	130
	12.2	Influence, reception, effect	132
	12.3	Pestalozzi and the moral discourse of teacher education in the United States	136
	12.4	History, education, and redemption	139
References			144
Index			165

Acknowledgments

I owe particular thanks to Sevcan Ekici, Rebekka Horlacher, and Claire Wolfson, who read the manuscript of the book and gave me thoughtful feedback that, I hope, improved the quality and readability of it. I am also very much obliged to Ellen Russon, who did an amazing job translating the manuscript. I especially thank William F. Pinar who encouraged me to publish this book in Palgrave Pivot, and I thank the two associate editors at Palgrave Macmillan, Sarah Nathan and Scarlet Neath, who provided the best possible guidance through the whole process.

palgrave▸pivot

www.palgrave.com/pivot

1
The Educationalization of Social Problems Around 1800

Abstract: *Johann Heinrich Pestalozzi is the star of a specific cultural shift that occurred around 1800 and that can be labeled an "educational turn." This educational turn describes a development that occurred in Northern and Western Europe as well as in the United States of America, when variously perceived problems came to be interpreted as educational problems. This phenomenon, the educationalization of social problems, became discursively established towards the end of the eighteenth century and then led to the foundation of the modern school in the context of the nation-states during the nineteenth century. Today, it continues unabated and finds expression in the framework of the World Bank, the United Nations, UNESCO, and the OECD. It is based on the premise that the central problems of the present and planning for the future are educational concerns.*

Tröhler, Daniel. *Pestalozzi and the Educationalization of the World.* New York: Palgrave Macmillan, 2013.
DOI: 10.1057/9781137346858.

For more than 150 years, Johann Heinrich Pestalozzi (1746–1827) was held to be the founding father of the modern school. Even if this conviction is no longer shared as often and as unreservedly today, it has persisted largely unscathed in our collective memory. In this collective memory there is in addition to Pestalozzi a forerunner, also from Switzerland: Jean-Jacques Rousseau (1712–1778) of Geneva. Rousseau is seen as responsible, in his novel *Emile* (Rousseau, 1762/1979), for revolutionizing educational thinking through an extensive orientation toward the child and the child's needs, whereas Pestalozzi is thought to have channeled this previously untamed revolution into modern schooling and to have disseminated it throughout Europe.

Starting in the late nineteenth century, this genesis of modern education and the modern school was told to many generations of teachers all over the world, and it was repeated in various forms in the textbooks used in teacher education. The narrative is incorrect, however, as more recent research has amply documented. In the case of Rousseau, the question has been raised again and again (and as early as in 1766; see Cajot, 1766)—and even more often in Rousseau's anniversary year of 2012—as to how revolutionary the Genevan actually was or whether he was not (also) a great compiler and plagiarist. As for Pestalozzi, it is now well-documented that he did not develop any theory of the modern school and did not head any educational institution resembling the modern school, that he did not play any crucial role in the development of the modern curriculum, and that he did not develop any learning method that proved to be practically implementable. And particularly important: Pestalozzi's central focus was certainly not on professional teachers but instead on mothers, in their loving relationship with the small child. Is it not then a paradox that the discipline "education," developed for teacher education since the mid-nineteenth century, was based so strongly on Pestalozzi? This book will deal with this question by narrating an intellectual biography of Pestalozzi against the background of a dramatically changing political, social, economic, and intellectual context that caused the need for an educational turn. Hence, the biography will not start with the birth of the hero but with an interpretation of a time that is (too) often simplified using the label "Enlightenment."

1.1   Pestalozzi and the educational turn

This book is about the paradox that education was developed as a discipline for teacher education starting in the mid-nineteenth century and was based strongly on Pestalozzi and his educational theory that focused on mothers. It defends the results of more recent research showing that Pestalozzi should not be called the founder of the modern school, at least not in the way that the great narrative would have us believe. It is true that the modern schools in Europe were established during Pestalozzi's lifetime or shortly thereafter: in the Netherlands and in Denmark there was a new, pioneering school law in 1814, in Norway in 1827, in Switzerland from 1831 on, in France in 1833, in Belgium and Sweden in 1842, and in Luxembourg in 1843, and the other European countries followed over the next decades. These modern schools were very different from the schools of the Ancien Régime; they were state-run, public, and much more secular than the old schools of the eighteenth century. They tried to reach all children to educate them to become citizens, and they had teachers that had been trained for their occupation by the state. The transition from the old to the new school did not take place from one day to the next, of course, but towards the end of the nineteenth century, the public school was a firmly established part and an important pillar of the nation-states. General compulsory school attendance was known, the school was usually free of cost, and its actors, the teachers, were prepared for their occupation systematically and certified accordingly. In their teacher training they acquired knowledge of the school subjects and the art of teaching them and dealt with pedagogy and education, and as appointed teachers they possessed a growing self-awareness with which they put forward their interests in institutions, associations, and labor unions. This successful development was accompanied by an incontestable revered figure to whom one could always successfully refer: Pestalozzi.

But why is the narrative of Pestalozzi as founding father of the modern school an untrue story? And if it is a false account, why is it worth dealing with Pestalozzi? Pestalozzi indeed had an important role in the founding of the modern school—however, not as founder and developer but instead as a figurehead within a sweeping cultural change that can be called the educational turn. This educational turn describes an evolution that occurred in Northern and Western Europe as well as in the United States of America between the middle of the eighteenth and the first third of the nineteenth century, when variously perceived social problems came to be interpreted as *educational* problems. This phenomenon, the educationalization of social problems, became discursively established towards the end of the eighteenth century and then led to the foundation of the modern school in the context of the nation-states in the nineteenth century. Today, this phenomenon continues unabated and finds expression in the framework of the World Bank, the United Nations, UNESCO, and the OECD. It is based on the premise that the central problems of the present and planning for the future are in fact basically educational concerns.

Not only did Pestalozzi not found the modern school, but he also was not the initiator of this cultural transformation process that educationalized the world. He can be seen as a major intensifier or catalyst of this phenomenon in his time. As the result of a set of contextual conditions—dramatic economic, political, and ideological events such as the American Revolution and the French Revolution—and specific personal characteristics, Pestalozzi became the unsurpassed standard-bearer of this transformation, reinforcing its fundamental assumptions. Undoubtedly he is the star of this cultural upheaval; through charisma, propaganda, and great rhetoric he anticipated the latent needs of times that had become uncertain around 1800 and made educational promises that seemed to reassure people. These people were monarchs, aristocrats, senior officials, philanthropists, and ambitious parents in half of Europe and the New World. A short time later, when the modern elementary schools were in fact founded following the developments after the Congress of Vienna (1814–1815), they did not rely on Pestalozzi's educational model, but they followed the educational reflex that Pestalozzi had propagated and reinforced so incomparably—namely, the reflex of interpreting social problems as *educational* problems. In this sense—and in this sense only—they were all Pestalozzians, and the teachers who through the course of the nineteenth century advanced from a rather ostracized to a respected occupation were not afraid to praise Pestalozzi successfully as their patron saint. Pestalozzi was the discursive hinge that connected teachers with persons in positions of political and cultural power, and that successfully lent legitimacy to teachers' demand for higher status and better working conditions.

1.2 The prehistory of the educational turn[1]

Up to the mid-eighteenth century, it was not at all "normal" to interpret perceived problems educationally—that is, to assign the solving of the problems to educational practice. Of course, there had always been conceptions of the political or social organization of people in which education played an important role. For example, Plato's *Republic* (Plato, 1966) can be read as the first great political model in which the achievement of social justice is tied to a detailed educational program. Still, up to the mid-eighteenth century there was no educationalized culture at all to speak of—that is, a culture that always viewed the big problems and challenges (also or even mainly) as educational problems and challenges. But what then made this educational turn possible?

This development had very specific requirements that had little to do with education; the increased educational reflexes were reactions to problems originally perceived as non-educational. What was decisive for the educational turn were changes in the way that people thought about two fundamental things in interpreting their lives: first, how people imagined history and development, and second, how they viewed the relation between money and politics. Both of these transformations, which remain important today, occurred around 1700 and replaced older perceptions and core notions that went back to the ancient world. They indicate the transformation of the early modern period in history to the modern period. The first of these transitions (history and development) was initiated in France, the second (money and politics) in England.

The transformations in the perception of history and development were initiated in France at the court of the King Louis XIV in Versailles, when the ancients' way of looking at things came under attack in the "quarrel of the Ancients and the Moderns."[2] Whereas up to the end of the seventeenth century, time and thus history had been seen, in analogy to the seasons, as an eternal cycle of events, in the eighteenth century a linear way of thinking ("progress") came to prevail that was oriented towards the future and in which outcomes were open (DeJean, 1997). At first, around 1680, this optimism applied only to progress in the sciences, but soon after, progress was seen also as a social and political program: Humanity would develop progressively towards peace, justice, and bliss, and political conditions that impeded this progress had to be violently destroyed. This was the justification for the French Revolution of 1789. The most impressive interpretation of this rational thinking on progress is probably that in *Outlines of an Historical View of the Progress of the Human Mind* (Condorcet, 1795/1796) by Marie Jean Antoine Nicolas de Caritat, Marquis de Condorcet (1743–1794), who was a philosopher, mathematician, politician, and educational reformer.[3] According to

Condorcet's interpretation, the French Revolution was the gateway to humanity's final great developmental epoch.

The second transformation (and second condition of the educational turn) has to do with the relation of money to politics, which changed towards the end of the seventeenth century at first in England. Up to that time, an ideal had prevailed in Europe according to which dispassionate reason was supposed to guide politics. At the same time, the commercial economy had been considered to be something "lower" or "baser," because it was accused of diverting attention and interest away from the common good and exposing people to the passionate pursuit of profit: in this ideology, calm, rational governing was seen as good and passion-driven money-making as bad. But around 1700 and to the present day, this system of reasoning is lost, not least because the commercial economy had become a social fact and actually important for politics. This ideological bias—the idea of dispassionate reason as a condition of good politics and the actual importance of the discredited commerce, connected to passions—had to be solved in order to legitimate the systems of political power, which depended more and more on money (for instance, for covering the rising costs of the massive expansion of administration or for the standing armies with their mercenaries).[4]

The problem to redefine the relation between money and politics was, in other words, the great financial difficulties of the European rulers, especially the English, who experienced a deep financial crisis towards 1700.[5] If the Kingdom of Great Britain[6] wanted to remain stable at home and be seen as a global power abroad, it had to obtain money. With no public funds (taxes) available, Scottish trader William Patterson (1658–1719)[7] proposed that wealthy private citizens found an association of subscribers (creditors).[8] Based on this initiative, the famous Bank of England was founded in 1694 and with it a successful and enduring system of public underwriting that from then on made it possible for individuals and companies to invest in the state (Dickson, 1970) and to meld money (private interest) and politics.[9]

The two transformations—first, notions of progress and the future replacing the theory of historical cycles, and second, the abolishing of the dividing line between politics and capital—did not only find enthusiastic supporters, they also gave rise to existential uncertainty, critique, and debates. One of these debates in the end led to the educational turn mentioned above in which Pestalozzi would play an impressive role.

1.3 Commercial progress vs. classical ideal of virtue

The most important reaction to the capitalization of politics, in a world that seemed all of a sudden to be driving progressively into an open and unknown future, was the revival of a political ideal that in research is called classical republicanism or civic humanism. This political ideal had roots in ancient political philosophy, was brought back to life in humanism in Florence around 1500, and formed the political background of the Reformation in Zurich after 1520. Later, this ideal shaped the founding of the Commonwealth of England (1649–1660) as well as the Puritans, who emigrated to the American colonies, and it was particularly revived in the founding years of the United States of America (Pocock, 1975; Wood, 1969). It is a firmly anti-monarchist—that is, republican—and anti-capitalist political ideal in which the citizens virtuously stand up for the common good. Their only passion is patriotism, love of the fatherland and its laws, which the citizens themselves have issued in self-government.

In England, it was the Whigs that rang in the commercial society, melding without any hesitation commercial economy and politics. In contrast, the Tories, the political opposition, propagated polemically the ideal of anti-capitalist classical republicanism. In the Tories' language of classical republicanism, the Whigs were doing nothing else than helping along political corruption, which the Tories opposed with their ideal of the virtuous citizen (Pocock, 1985), who was ideally a landowner.[10] The idea was that landowners were less passionate than commercial men because they needed to be far less concerned about income than people who invested their money in unstable stock markets and were therefore nervous and in constant worry over their investments: the tulip mania,[11] the first extensive speculative bubble in economic history, causing great losses in the Netherlands in 1637, was definitely present in the collective memory around 1700: money traders distraught with concern to maximize profits could not possibly be good politicians. Only landowners were in a position to put themselves fully in the service of the common good:

> The landed man, successor to the master of the classical *oikos*, was permitted the leisure and autonomy to consider what was to others' good as well as his own; but the individual engaged in exchange could discern only particular values – that of the commodity which was his, that of the commodity for which he exchanged it. (Pocock, 1975, p. 464)

This condemnation of the commercial man and glorification of the landed man was not at all restricted to England. It was an international phenomenon that also influenced the United States, as shown, for example, by Thomas Jefferson who as a matter of course linked the ideal of the citizen to agriculture just as he connected wars to commerce and self-interest: "I repeat it again, cultivators of the earth are the most virtuous and independent citizens (...) But the actual habits of our countrymen attach them to commerce. They will exercise it for themselves. Wars then must sometimes be our lot" (Jefferson, 1785, 1787/1984, p. 301).

However, the advancement of the commercial society could also not be halted by the blossoming of the ideal of the republican citizen. The natural sciences produced know-how for farming methods in agriculture, and surplus products were exported. Technical advances simplified the production of goods, trade flourished, and the capitalist bourgeoisie pushed for more political influence, especially in France, which ultimately would lead to the outbreak of the French Revolution in 1789. On the other hand, over the course of the eighteenth century the political ideal of the anti-capitalist citizen committed to the common good became increasingly attractive. The two opposing ideals were the central issue in a large part of the famous debates between the Federalists and the anti-Federalists concerning the Constitution of the United States. And it was not by chance that some anonymous contributions to the debates were written under the pseudonyms "Caesar" (traitor of the Roman Republic) and "Cato" (defender of the Roman Republic) (Bailyn, 1993).

1.4 Reformed Protestantism and the educational strengthening of the soul

In the second half of the eighteenth century, the contradiction between progress in science and the economy on the one hand, and the popularity of the ideal of the anti-capitalist citizen on the other, led to attempts to reconcile the two positions. It was not by chance that this reconciliation was pursued effectively in the Protestant strongholds of Switzerland, with the Republic of Zurich, Pestalozzi's birthplace, especially leading the way. Protestantism—notwithstanding its different denominations—had turned from the Catholic emphasis on the institution (the Holy Mother Church) to the individual's soul as the instance of salvation with no fundamental need of consecrated mediators (priests) between

God and the individual. This Protestant focus on the individual's soul became the starting point of the educationalization of the world, in so far as the soul became the central object of education. The difference between German Protestantism (Lutheranism) and Swiss Reformed Protestantism (Zwinglianism and Calvinism) led to two different educational ideologies. Whereas Luther's unworldly political and social ideology led to the political indifferent and contemplative educational ideology of *Bildung*,[12] Swiss Reformed Protestantism developed an educational program heading at active citizenship as a reaction to these fundamental transformations.

This attempt at reconciliation of classical republicanism and progress in Swiss Reformed Protestantism is evident in an explosive case of censorship in Zurich in 1763–1764, when Pestalozzi was 17 years old. It occurred in response to a translation into German of Gabriel Bonnot de Mably's[13] (1763) *Entretiens de Phocion*, an anti-capitalist tract that was a plea for an agrarian republic. The translator of the work into German, Hans Conrad Vögelin of Zurich, came into conflict with the censor because of a passage in which Phocion,[14] in accordance with agrarian republicanism and its ideal of the landed man, espouses the opinion that tradesmen should not be allowed to participate in government, as they tend to be unjust and selfish (Mably, 1764, p. 109). The censor objected to this passage because it was "directly opposed" to Zurich's economic structures (Vögelin, cited in Zehnder-Stadlin, 1875, p. 664), in which the crafts, early industry, and trade were essential. For this reason, Vögelin then added a note to the German translation stating that the corruption of the tradesmen noted by Phocion did not lie in the trades *per se*. There was no reason why a tradesman could not be virtuous: "Why should they not be industrious and moderate, why should they not be able to have a desire for fame and religion?" And opposing the opinion that agriculture was a considerably more favorable basis for the republic than the trades, Vögelin wrote, "What then is especially virtuous about the plow, more so than the hammer of the blacksmith?" Regarding Phocion's criticism of tradesmen Vögelin concluded: "The nobility are good, tradesmen are good, and commerce is also good, as long as it can be 'correctly modified'" (Vögelin, cited in Mably, 1764, p. 111).

This idea of modification, or making virtuous, was interpreted as *inner strengthening*—that is, as strengthening of the soul, as inner strength. This idea subsequently became the starting point of the educationalization of the world, for it meant that a person with sufficient inner virtue could safely resist all temptations of the (commercial) world and be a virtuous and active citizen. Here, inner strength represented the Protestant internalization of the steadfast Roman warrior hero, fighting no so much the enemy in the battlefield but rather the inner enemy of selfish passion. It was to be expressed as republican virtue in the time of commercialization, interlacing in this way the common good and commercial society, and thereby shaping the future for the welfare of all.

This modification—that is, strengthening of the soul towards (civic) virtue—was the program that was to be realized through education. This is illustrated paradigmatically by an essay (Iselin, 1781) written by one of the most important Swiss intellectuals of the eighteenth century, Isaak Iselin (1728–1882), council secretary of Basel, who precisely at the time was of great importance to Pestalozzi and who supported Pestalozzi with the publication of his first and very successful novel *Lienhard und Gertrud* (1781). In Iselin's (1781) work, *Schreiben eines Vaters an seinen Sohn, der sich der Handelschaft widmet* [Letter of a Father to His Son Who is Devoted to Trade], in agreement with classical republicanism, the occupation of farmer is depicted as especially noble, but following closely in second place is the occupation of merchant. Iselin warns his son against choosing to be a merchant simply in order to enjoy privately the "pleasures and delicacies." Iselin then advises his son to apply the "eight principles" that underlie *any* occupation—including the occupation of merchant (pp. 392f.). To ensure that his son always submits to these good intentions (pp. 420ff.), Iselin provides a supplement at the end of the essay, outlining a procedure of self-examination designed to serve "Preparation in the Morning. Examination in the Evening." Following this procedure, Iselin's son was to start the day by recalling his great duties to God and humanity and by recalling Reason, which makes him in God's image. Only insights into goodness and beauty should adorn his soul. He should treat the poor well, fight against the depravities, and refrain from pride and malice. He was to treat women respectfully and not harass them with criminal passions; hard work, moderation, gentleness, and justice should be his central virtues. He was to avoid vanity and garrulousness, and likewise hedonism and flattery: "Seek the company of the virtuous, wise, and learned" (p. 423). Then in the evening, his son should ask himself the following questions: "From what fault have you freed yourself today? What evil have you conquered? To what extent have you improved your soul?" (p. 425).

Educating the young towards self-examination thus appeared as the key to the resolution of the conflict between republican politics and the modern economy, as guarantor of an ordered modernity that does not fall prey to the passions but instead is meant to ensure the common good *and* progress. In the educational program, the solution was based primarily on strengthening the soul and less on acquiring knowledge: Those who—through education—could strengthen the souls of the children did not have to fear the open-ended and uncertain future. It is this idea that is at the origin of the educational turn, this great transformation process that educationalized the world in a lasting way. Many persons had a part in shaping and popularizing this transformation, but none were as influential as Johann Heinrich Pestalozzi, who through his lifetime became the great promoter of an educationalized world. Just how he came to take on this role and how he left his mark on it will be traced in the following chapters.

Notes

1 For a more detailed presentation of this and the next section below, see (Tröhler, 2011b).
2 http://en.wikipedia.org/wiki/Quarrel_of_the_Ancients_and_the_Moderns
3 http://en.wikipedia.org/wiki/Marquis_de_Condorcet
4 To prevent misunderstanding, I must emphasize that capitalism was a far older phenomenon, as research studies by Le Goff (1956; 1986) have shown. But it is no coincidence that the advent of the notion of "capitalism" was in the second half of the eighteenth century (in French and English) or even nineteenth century (in German), as it indicates that this mode of economy had become in some way distinguishable and even conspicuous and, for cultural traditions, a specific ideological problem. In this sense, the Fugger banking family, which ran the first great lending house in history (in the fifteenth century), was also not an early phenomenon of the Bank of England, because the Fugger family always made loans on the basis of personal relationships with the monarchs. In contrast, through the Bank of England the relationship between lender and borrower became anonymous.
5 After the English Civil Wars, Cromwell's reign, and the violent religious conflicts, England was ruined when King William III and Queen Mary II took the throne together (coregency) in 1688, and the situation worsened again dramatically in 1690 when the Royal Navy lost the Battle of Beachy Head against France.

6 Strictly speaking, the unified Kingdom of Great Britain was founded only in 1706 by the Treaty of Union and in 1707 by the Acts of Union; previously, the monarchs were simply the rulers of the three different Kingdoms of England, Scotland, and Ireland.
7 http://en.wikipedia.org/wiki/William_Paterson_(banker)
8 In order to make a loan of £1.2m to the government at an interest rate of 8 %.
9 The owners of capital could now invest in the stability of a government and in doing so—depending on the success of the government's operations—expect a return (Pocock, 1985, p. 108). Political success became the success that would bring about the greatest financial gain. This commercial interest in politics "transformed the relation between government and citizens" and defined it as relations between debtors and creditors; "It was not the market, but the stock market, which precipitated an English awareness, about 1700, that political relations were on the verge of becoming capitalist relations" (Pocock, 1985, p. 110). It is no coincidence that at the time the notion of the passions, which prior to 1700 had strictly negative connotations, became increasingly neutralized and connected with the notion of interest, as shown by Felix Raab (1964) in *The English Face of Machiavelli: A Changing Interpretation, 1500–1700* and by Albert O. Hirschman (1977) in *The Passions and the Interests: Political Arguments for Capitalism Before Its Triumph*.
10 The accusation that the Whigs were fostering corruption was based on a specific psychological reasoning. According to the reproach, people whose social and political lives are shaped largely by trade and commercial economy could not be committed to the common good at all. Commercial men were specialists who were devoted to the production and trade of specific goods and who paid other specialists—politicians and soldiers (mercenaries)—to lead the country politically and militarily. From the view of the Tories or republican ideology, commercial men lacked true rationality, for they were subject to their passions for wealth: "For these the appropriate term in the republican lexicon was corruption" (Pocock 1975, p. 464). Against this, the patriotic and republican ideal was a fully moral person who was able and willing to fulfill all public duties. This ideal is not based on owners of money and goods but on owners of land.
11 "Tulip mania" refers to events concerning tulip bulbs and speculation in seventeenth-century Netherlands. The Dutch developed a passion for tulips, which were cultivated by the upper social classes of the bourgeoisie, scholars, and aristocrats. Around 1600, the tulip bulb trade became commercialized, which led to a massive price increase in the 1630s. Lured by the promise of big profits, ever more speculators entered the market, and prices became outlandish. The tulip market crashed utterly in February 1637, and the investments were lost (Dash, 1999).

12 Luther's theology emphasizes the inward freedom of the humans but is indifferent towards political freedom—and therefore receptive to totalitarian governments, as John Dewey (1915) bluntly emphasized in his lecture series *German Philosophy and Politics*. A short and concise analysis of the educational theory of this Lutheran ideology, *Bildung*, is provided by Rebekka Horlacher (Horlacher, 2012).

13 Gabriel Bonnot de Mably (1709–1785) was the older brother of Étienne Bonnot de Condillac (1715–1780); they both belong to the leading French intellectuals of the eighteenth century; see http://en.wikipedia.org/wiki/Gabriel_Bonnot_de_Mably

14 In the classical republican literature of the eighteenth century, it was customary to use ancient heroes as a mouthpiece. The most famous example is probably *Cato's Letters or Essays on Liberty, Civil and Religious, and Other Important Subjects*, a collection of republican essays by John Trenchard and Thomas Gordon (Trenchard & Gordon, 1995/1720–1723), written under the pseudonym "Cato." Cato the Younger (95–46 BC) was the great opponent of Caesar and was unbendable and steadfast concerning republican virtues. Mably's (1764) Phocion refers to a student of Plato's who defended republican principles industriously and incorruptibly.

2
Zurich Around 1750: Economic and Cultural Boom and Revolutionary Activities

Abstract: Zurich, the hometown of Pestalozzi, met the specific conditions in which this cultural shift, the educationalization of social problems, could emerge: it was a republic with limited democracy (limited to male citizens of the city), and it was a stronghold of Reformed Protestantism. The blend of republicanism and Protestantism brought forth both an increased skepticism towards processes of capitalization of society and a vision according to which the uncertain social developments should be secured by the strengthening of children's souls. The conviction was that a well-educated soul would be steadfast in the face of the seductions of a capitalized society. This conviction is the key expression of the educational turn—that is, the educationalization of social problems. As a result of these developments and conditions, Zurich experienced an outbreak of youth unrest in which the young Pestalozzi would be socialized after 1760.

Tröhler, Daniel. *Pestalozzi and the Educationalization of the World*. New York: Palgrave Macmillan, 2013.
DOI: 10.1057/9781137346858.

In Zurich the central requirements for an educational turn existed: Zurich was a republic with limited democracy (limited to male citizens of the city), and it was a stronghold of Reformed Protestantism.[1] Around 1750, the signs of commercialization of society became increasingly evident and this led—as it did in England around 1700—to a revival of the republican anti-commercial ideal. But in contrast to England with its Anglican Church, in Protestant Zurich the ideal of virtue extolled by republicanism became quickly educationalized. Pestalozzi was affected by this early wave of republican educationalism and was socialized as a young student in a revolutionary republican youth movement.

2.1 The political organization of the Republic of Zurich in the eighteenth century

Like numerous other territories of Switzerland prior to the outbreak of the Helvetic Revolution in 1798, Zurich was a republican city-state like the ancient Greek city-states or the city-states of Renaissance Italy. A city-state was usually made up of a city with free citizens protected within its walls and surrounding territory, the inhabitants of which had far fewer freedoms than the city citizens and who were mainly meant to supply the citizens of the city with agricultural goods and serve as soldiers in case of military conflicts (whereas the citizens would be officers). During the course of the eighteenth century, through targeted city power politics, the gap between the freedom and rights of the city citizens and the inhabitants of the countryside had widened noticeably. This privileged status of the city citizens was raised even higher by the fact that starting in the early 1700s no more immigrated families obtained Zurich city citizenship. As a result, through the course of the eighteenth century a very few families came to power that had made fortunes especially through trade, whereby many of the goods were produced in cottage industry in the countryside. This "oligarchization" of the social conditions contradicted the intentions of the Zurich constitution, the origins of which go back to the fourteenth century. This difference between the historical ideal of the constitution and the current day became the starting point for criticism of the conditions, which led to a radical youth movement after 1760.

From around 1500 up to the Helvetic Revolution in 1798, the constitution of Zurich remained mostly unchanged; it provided for a kind of republican aristo-democracy, a combination of republic, aristocracy, and democracy.² According to the aristocratic principle, not all male inhabitants of the territory were eligible to be elected; only a limited selection of inhabitants were eligible—namely, citizens of the city. To be a citizen of Zurich, one had to be either a member of a guild or a descendant of one of the few noble families that were organized in their own society, called the *Constaffel*. Within this elitist framework there was a democratic principle insofar as each guild as well as the Constaffel elected its delegates, who were assembled in the grand council (*Grosser Rat*) of Zurich and thus formed the parliament. A part of the grand council was also the little council (*Kleiner Rat*), whose members were the guild masters; unlike the grand council, they met every day and accordingly had far more extensive authority. Within this select circle, there was also a secret council (*Geheimer Rat*), which advised on delicate matters, both domestic and foreign. At the very top there were two mayors, elected by the council and taking turns serving for six months of the year.

Especially the arrangement with two alternating mayors makes it clear that Zurich saw itself as a republic. Usually, the term republic describes a form of government in which the citizens call themselves "free"—that is, they themselves can legislate (create laws). As it was always expected that people having too much power could abuse their power for private purposes and exploit the people, monarchy was rejected, including elective monarchy. Selfish monarchs were called "corrupt" as well as "tyrants," and the opposite of the tyrant was the virtuous, free citizen, who was disposed to promote the common good. This ideal was not limited to Zurich but rather was cultivated in all Reformed Protestant and republican contexts, even by John Adams (1735–1826), the second President of the United States of America. In view of the heated debates on the Declaration of Independence, Adams wrote the following to Mercy Otis Warren (1728–1814)³ on April 16, 1776: "There must be a positive Passion for the public good, the public Interest, Honour, Power, and Glory, established in the Minds of the People, or there can be no Republican Government, nor any real Liberty; and this public Passion must be Superior to all private Passions" (Adams, cited in Stourzh, 1970, p. 65).⁴

Zurich's understanding of the republic was reflected not only in the two mayors, which limited the power of the highest authority, but also in the fact that on the day of elections to the grand council, the guild members—the voting body—had to swear an oath to elect only the most skilled and the best—that is, to elect citizens with a demonstrated record of service to the fatherland. This makes a republic also a meritocracy, in which people are not elected because they come from a famous family or are extremely wealthy, but rather because they deserve to be granted power due to their great contributions to the fatherland. From the perspective of classical virtue republicanism, a lot of money and luxury is an expression of egotism and political and moral decline. This republican way of thinking shaped Zurich for centuries, and it was dramatically reactivated in the eighteenth century when critical contemporaries noticed that Zurich had in fact become massively commercialized.

2.2 Commercialization of societal life in Zurich around 1750

The constitution of Zurich and the republican way of thinking were one side of life in Zurich in the eighteenth century, and the actual economic and societal developments were the other. Starting in the mid-1600s, mayors were no longer craftsmen but were usually rich businessmen or sons of influential families who had climbed the career ladder rapidly in the guilds. Decisive in this connection was also a new law at the beginning of the eighteenth century that lifted the previous restriction that only eldest sons could succeed their fathers in the guilds. From then on, it was possible to choose one's guild, including guilds that had nothing to do with the traditional occupation of a family's forefathers. Influential families could now send not only the oldest son into the father's guild, but several sons into the various guilds, thereby extending the possibility of successful political careers to a greater number of their male descendants. In this way, influential families could increase their power even more.

But it was not just various new laws—the massive preference granted to the city citizens over the inhabitants of the surrounding countryside, the abolishment of the option for new families to become citizens, free choice of guilds for city citizens—that promoted the oligarchization of the city but rather also a long phase of steady population growth and continuous development of Zurich's industry (mainly production and trade of spinning mills products and woven goods). As the goods produced in cottage industry in the countryside around 1750 were mainly produced by hand, little investment was required of the city industrialists. This development, which had been spared any larger crises, and in addition a system of duties and charges resulted in a lot of money not only for a few families but for the entire city around 1750. The great wealth of the city of Zurich stood in contrast to the scarce finances of the monarchies abroad, which cultivated an extremely costly lifestyle in the eighteenth century—Versailles, the court of the French king, was the role model imitated by all of the monarchies—and had developed a great need for money, not least for their standing mercenary armies. With the strong demand for capital abroad and Zurich's full coffers, the city authorities began to think about exporting capital. In 1754 the government of Zurich established a "committee to oversee return on investments," headed by Johann Jacob Leu, which was the origins of Zurich's Bank Leu, which was merged into Credit Suisse in 2006.[5] This interest rate committee raised monies, at first from the various city coffers and later also from private parties, at an interest rate of 3 to 3.5 percent. With the aim to earn a higher return, these monies were invested in loans to foreign powers and also in loans to trading companies and plantations in Middle and South America.[6]

Like with the Bank of England in 1694, these government-initiated allocations of monies were connected with something that was decisively new. Prior to 1750, namely, the giving of credit had been concentrated mainly on interested parties of the same political or religious persuasion. These were foremost "endangered" villages or even estates around Zurich that had been ensnared by the Catholic Church and that through loans were to be brought back into dependency on and loyalty to Protestantism. A few loans had been made to large cities, but Zurich had been restrained in the case of France, which favored the Catholic parts of Switzerland. This system had been characterized by direct loans to lords and princes, communities, or also private persons and was dependent not least on personal contacts; it was a "personal" kind of business. This characteristic ended with the work of the interest rate committee, and the age of the impersonal system of loans began. The political and religious dimension of lending retreated into the background, and business was now conducted with more or less any interested party, regardless of that party's political and ideological preferences, as long as it could show creditworthiness. Profiting from this changed practice was not least countries such as France, towards which Zurich had previously been cautious for political reasons. The only condition now was the creditor's supposed ability to pay and the expected interest profit. With this, the monetary and credit system had freed itself from the grip of the Zurich republic and had become "capitalistic."

This commercialization of official policy and then of private banking activities had parallels in social and cultural life. The changes were especially evident in the intensified construction of new buildings, comprising both a quantitative increase and an aesthetic reorientation. The most striking example occurred with the decision taken by the *Zunft zur Meisen*, a politically very influential and financially powerful guild, who decided to build a new guild house in 1751. Under the influence of Austrian and French architecture, the builder broke with Zurich's traditions of relatively anonymous buildings and built a winged construction in the Rococo style. The facade was in the Austrian-Bohemian style, which gave the building a special, and for Zurich extremely foreign, appeal.[7] In spite of the skepticism or outrage that the new building elicited, further magnificent buildings were built in the following years, also for private parties. The commercialization of Zurich life had become visible and thus open to criticism. The keyword of the criticism was "luxury," which since Antiquity had been associated with softening, feminization, and the passions and which stood diametrically opposed to the male ideal of political-military virtue.

Out of this fundamental criticism the republican language was revived, and thus the ideal of patriotic virtue was publicly extolled. From the question as to how virtue could develop in a corrupt context, new educational concepts emerged. If young people could no longer be socialized in an existing virtuous context then they would have to be specifically educated in the virtues.

2.3   The fight against corruption and decline

The commercialization of societal life in the eighteenth century was accompanied by the oligarchization of city society, and both were viewed—in the eyes of the advocates of the idea of a virtuous republic—as necessarily connected to one another. The two phenomena appeared to reflect the removal from the basic principles and historical foundations of the free republic of Zurich, as specific indicators of the decline of the free state, the emergence of corrupt favoritism, and the reign of egoistic capitalists devoid of all patriotism. Zurich the free and proud republic seemed to be in serious peril, and this elicited a variety of reactions and criticisms.

Criticism of the developments in Zurich carried strong historical and idealizing undertones. The changes were depicted as the fall of a once strong and virtuous dim and distant past, as a betrayal of the virtuous forefathers—that is, betrayal of the heroes in the struggles for Swiss freedom in the fourteenth century, who in the eyes of the critics had selflessly and fraternally lost their lives for the freedom of the fatherland. This retrospection to the age of heroes of the old Swiss Confederation came from a historian who taught at the Zurich Academy, Johann Jacob Bodmer (1698-1783).[8] Bodmer—who became Pestalozzi's most important teacher at the Zurich Academy—had an outstanding reputation in Europe, not so much for his historiography as for his critical contribution to letters and poetry, advocating a style of poetry affecting the souls of the readers in a moral and practical way, so that letters and poetry had a practical, purifying effect.

Bodmer had earned his reputation around 1740 along with his friend and colleague, Johann Jacob Breitinger (1701-1776), in a literary dispute with Johann Christoph Gottsched (1700-1766), a German author and critic and son of a Lutheran pastor. The conflict was conducted publicly and made great waves.[9] Due to Bodmer and other famous Zurich literary figures and artists, such as poet and painter Salomon Gessner (1730-1788)[10] and agricultural reformer, author, and city physician Johann Caspar Hirzel (1725-1803),[11] Zurich had become a mecca for a new understanding of the cultural and social role of aesthetics and attracted many aesthetes and intellectuals mainly from Germany: Friedrich Gottlieb Klopstock (1824-1803) and Christoph Martin Wieland (1733-1813)[12] were attracted to Zurich, as were also Ewald Christian von Kleist (1715-1759)[13] and somewhat later Johann Gottlieb Fichte (1762-1814)[14] and Christoph Meiners (1748-1810),[15] who saw in Zurich the "Athens of the North."

Bodmer's practical-political understanding of history was derived from a strong identification with the Swiss struggles for freedom in the fourteenth century, when—according to legend—the determined, freedom-loving Swiss had freed themselves from the superior strength of the Austrian occupying forces owing to their patriotic virtue, fraternity, and steadfastness. For Bodmer, compared to these fighters for liberty, the men in his day had grown soft and were selfish because of commerce, which was putting the free republic at risk. Bodmer utilized his position as a professor at the Zurich Academy and read Montesquieu's *De l'Esprit des Loix* (Montesquieu, 1748)[16] with his students, in which Montesquieu describes how luxury and wealth had always undermined the republics and exposed them to decay and decline. As Bodmer found his students' fathers' generation to be corrupted—that is, to have been exposed to the passions for riches and fame—Bodmer strove to educate a new generation of steadfast republican heroes, who in political office would one day bring the city of Zurich back to republican glory.

Bodmer gathered together some of his most talented students—all of them between the ages of 17 and 22—and alongside their studies, read and discussed with them, in his home, key ancient and modern political works and Swiss history, which reinforced them in their opinion that Zurich was on the verge of falling apart. Bodmer himself began to write dramas about medieval heroes, which were read by the students. The high point was the publication in 1762 of Bodmer's play, *Die gerechte Zusammenschwörung* [The Just Oath], the first William Tell drama of the eighteenth century in German language, which depicted the cruelty of the tyrant, Gessler, particularly vividly and which culminated in a defense of the murder of the tyrant by William Tell.[17] Encouraged in their enthusiasm by Bodmer's reading matter and other works on the great freedom fighters of the ancient world and the Swiss struggles for freedom in the fourteenth century, the young students began to call themselves "patriots" and "sons of Sparta." They were determined, in republican steadfastness, to fight the inconsistencies and injustices in the city of Zurich and, regardless of their personal fates, to save the city from further decline. They also met without their father figure Bodmer in various places and in part secret youth circles and societies and forged plans for actively intervening in politics, which at their young age they could not do at all legally. In 1762 the time had come for practical implementation of the republican criticism of the city of Zurich, which the most radical of the students called "revolution" to distinguish it from "reform." Pestalozzi was to play an important part in this radical movement.

2.4 The republican youth movement in Zurich after 1760

The republican dissatisfaction resulted from analysis of the political and social present day in Zurich. It was seen as a decline, caused by commerce, of the once model republic of Zurich. This not only triggered intensive intellectual study of the relevant literature from Xenophon to

Montesquieu but also led a number of especially republican minded students to meet in half-secret circles. Here they discussed what actions might save the city of Zurich from its fall. Based on their ideal of the fearless, steadfast, and virtuous citizen, they believed that they had been called to uncover the worst evils of the city, in the hope that in this way the city could then recover. They believed that they knew of enough examples of corrupt powerful people, who were to be driven out of the republic. The "corrupt" power holders became the targets of the activities of the young sons of Sparta, who denounced their misdemeanors—a courageous strategy for young men not yet eligible to be citizens in an age of political censorship of the press.

The very first case of public condemnation of corrupt discharge of public office ended in a massive disruption of public life in Zurich. Two young theology students were involved who would later attain extraordinary fame: the later painter Johann Heinrich Füssli (1841–1825), who in London under the name Henry Fusely and was soon to have a decisive influence in the art world,[18] and the later preacher Johann Caspar Lavater (1741–1801), who would attain great fame in Europe with his book *Physiognomische Fragmente* (1775–1778) (Essays on Physiognomy).[19] In the summer of 1762 Füssli and Lavater had sent an anonymous letter to a land administrator (bailiff) named Felix Grebel (1714–1787), who was the son-in-law of one of the two reigning mayors in the city of Zurich, demanding that he make compensation for his exploitative and extortionate administration. When, over the course of the next few months, the accused bailiff did not find it necessary to respond, Füssli and Lavater brought the issue to the public. But the public accusation was directed not only at Grebel but also—and this was very courageous in the face of the censorship of the time—at the political elite of the city of Zurich that had shielded the bailiff for so long. Accordingly, Füssli and Lavater distributed to prominent members of parliament a leaflet with the title "The Unjust Landvogt: Or, Complaints of a Patriot about the Unjust Government." The leaflet mentioned the term tyrant and also praised the Roman tyrant killer, Brutus.[20]

This action caused turmoil in the city. All the same, the city investigated the case of Grebel, who escaped prosecution by fleeing the country. The two anonymous authors of the leaflet were asked to report to the authorities, which they staunchly did. As Lavater and Füssli were also sons of very influential families, they could be assured of a relatively mild penalty. They were strongly reprimanded and told to leave the country for a year-long "educational stay" abroad—the object being to calm things down as quickly as possible. Füssli never returned to Zurich at all (except for short-term visits); he traveled on to London, where he began his successful carrier as an artist. His paintings of the old Swiss history of freedom, including especially the *Rütlischwur*,[21] are still held today to be the epitome of the heroic admiration for the founding of Switzerland. Despite the hasty departure from Zurich of the two "perpetrators" in January 1763, their influence was considerable; and in the circle of other, somewhat younger "patriots," the two became the undisputed heroes of the republican revolution against what they still called the corrupt city of Zurich. Lavater and Füssli were particularly admired by the members of the "Moral Political and Historical Society," founded on July 1, 1762, by young theology students between the ages of 17 and 22 who had also become politically aware in Bodmer's circle and aimed, through studying history, to contribute to moral and political improvement of the city of Zurich. Johann Heinrich Pestalozzi would become a member of this society two years after it had formed, in the summer of 1764, but it was soon dissolved on December 24, 1764.

Notes

1   Around 1500 many reform movements tried to reform the Catholic Church, which dominated not only religious life in today's sense but almost the totality of human existence. Of all these reform movements, three are still quite known today and go back to three reformers, one reformer in Germany (Martin Luther, 1483–1546) and two in Switzerland (Huldrych Zwingli (1484–1531) in Zurich, where Pestalozzi grew up, and Jean Calvin (1509–1564) in Geneva, where Jean-Jacques Rousseau grew up). These three reformers disagreed in many respects, and these differences still play a crucial role in today's educational discourse (see Tröhler, 2011a). The differences that matter in relation to education are less theological or metaphysical differences and more political-ethical differences. Whereas Luther's Protestantism remained largely restricted to the inwards sphere of human beings and their religiosity and not only excluded any political consequences but also accepted political injustice, Zwingli's Reformed Protestantism encompassed political and social reforms: Zwingli clearly rejected monarchies with their dangers of corruption and favored republics in which political authorities would rule the state but would be liable to render account to theologians. This Protestant-republican idea differed from that of Jean Calvin's (1509–1564),

the reformer in Geneva, who aimed at installing a theocracy in which the state's authority had a solely religious basis. Zwingli's political philosophy, and especially that of his young, like-minded companion, Heinrich Bullinger (1504–1575), would become important for the English dissenters and largely determined the political views of the English Pilgrims who emigrated to the American colonies in the seventeenth century.

2 The following overview of conditions in Zurich is based on Holzhey and Zurbuchen (1997), Peyer (1968), Wehrli (1989), and Wysling (1983).
3 Mercy Otis Warren was one of the most remarkable women in the shaping of the American republic in the second half of the eighteenth century; see http://en.wikipedia.org/wiki/Mercy_Otis_Warren
4 The republican citizen is in a certain sense a holistic person, who as a working person attends to feeding his family, as a politician attends to just laws for the common good, and as a soldier attends to defending the fatherland. In this classical image of the free citizen of the republic, which goes back to the ancient world, the political and military virtue of the citizen plays a decisive role, because it is that virtue that is to prevent him, in the execution of his political and military duties, from thinking too much of his family and his family's welfare. A citizen without this virtue quickly becomes corrupt—that is, he puts his personal well-being above the public welfare.
5 http://en.wikipedia.org/wiki/Bank_Leu
6 Success came quickly and was huge, so that in a very short period six private banks that operated according to the same model came into being in Zurich. Shortly after 1750, Zurich had become a financial center that was hard to reconcile with the idea of a virtuous republic.
7 See http://en.wikipedia.org/wiki/Zunfthaus_zur_Meisen. The guild, the *Zunft zur Meisen*, named after a house that carried the name of the bird *Meise* [titmouse], was founded in 1336 and was originally the guild of the skilled trades of coopers, saddlers, painters, and wine merchants.
8 http://en.wikipedia.org/wiki/Johann_Jakob_Bodmer
9 http://en.wikipedia.org/wiki/Johann_Christoph_Gottsched
10 http://en.wikipedia.org/wiki/Salomon_Gessner
11 http://en.wikipedia.org/wiki/Hans_Caspar_Hirzel
12 https://en.wikipedia.org/wiki/Christoph_Martin_Wieland
13 http://en.wikipedia.org/wiki/Ewald_Christian_von_Kleist
14 http://en.wikipedia.org/wiki/Johann_Gottlieb_Fichte
15 http://en.wikipedia.org/wiki/Christoph_Meiners
16 Montesquieu's *De l'Esprit des Loix* is one of the milestones of the eighteenth century. As early as in 1750 the first English translation was published (Montesquieu, 1750) in London by Thomas Nugent, who had become famous for the first travel guidebook on Europe, *The Grand Tour – Containing an*

Exact Description of Most of the Cities, Towns and Remarkable Places of Europe (Nugent, 1749).

17 The most famous literary version was written by Friedrich Schiller (Schiller, 1804); Gioachino Rossini wrote the opera of the same name in 1829.
18 Henry Fuseli—actually Heinrich Füssli—became one of the most famous painters of the eighteenth century (see http://en.wikipedia.org/wiki/Henry_Fuseli), and he also published a report (Fuseli, 1767) on Jean-Jacques Rousseau's unsuccessful stay in London that attracted a great deal of attention.
19 http://en.wikipedia.org/wiki/Johann_Kaspar_Lavater
20 It is reported that through his involvement in the murder of Caesar, Marcus Junius Brutus Caepio (85–42 BC), or Brutus for short, freed Rome from the king's rule and restored the republic.
21 According to legend, the *Rütlischwur*, the oath of the Old Swiss Confederacy taken on the Rütli meadow above Lake Lucerne, marked the heroic founding of free Switzerland in 1291 (see http://en.wikipedia.org/wiki/Rütlischwur). In 1780 Füssli painted the oath taking as a dramatic act (http://www.zeno.org/Kunstwerke/B/Füssli,+Johann+Heinrich%3A+Rütlischwur)

3
The Development and Early Fate of a Republican Revolutionary

Abstract: *Pestalozzi was 16 years old when the youth unrest in Zurich became visible in 1762. The same year saw the publication of Jean-Jacques Rousseau's* The Social Contract *and* Emile, or on Education, *which heated up cultural criticism in Europe and gave the young revolutionaries in Zurich additional impetus. In Zurich the years from 1762 to 1767 were marked by the youth movement that was oriented towards ancient republican ideals. The movement came to a standstill around 1767, because the political authorities massively restricted the protests and because the activists entered marriageable age, with their interests shifting accordingly. This was also the case for Pestalozzi, who was accepted into the circle of young patriots in 1764, became engaged to marry in 1767, and moved away from Zurich to—very much in the style of the republican ideal—learn about farming. In 1769 Pestalozzi married his betrothed, Anna Schulthess (1738–1815), and they bought farmland to become virtuous country people.*

Tröhler, Daniel. *Pestalozzi and the Educationalization of the World.* New York: Palgrave Macmillan, 2013.
DOI: 10.1057/9781137346858.

Pestalozzi grew up fatherless and in rather modest circumstances. He carried out his studies at the Zurich Acadamy and was especially concerned by the increasing ideological tensions between commerce and classical republicanism. As a student he became acquainted with the revolutionary youth movement and internalized its aims and visions maybe to a stronger degree than its initiators; this experience determined his near and later future to a considerable degree. In 1762, when Pestalozzi was a young man of 16 years of age, the appearance of youth unrest in Zurich coincided with the publications of Jean-Jacques Rousseau's *The Social Contract* (Rousseau, 1762/2002) and *Emile, or on Education* (Rousseau, 1762/1979). The importance of this momentous historical coincidence and the impact it would have on Pestalozzi must not be overlooked.

3.1 Pestalozzi's childhood and youth

Johann Heinrich Pestalozzi was born on January 12, 1746, as the third child of Johann Baptist Pestalozzi (1718–1751), a moderately successful surgeon who practiced without academic studies, and his wife Susanna Pestalozzi-Hotz (1720–1796). Although the Pestalozzi family had citizenship, their position in the social web of the city of Zurich was not very high. Johann Baptist's marriage in 1742 to Susanna Hotz, who came from the underprivileged countryside, rather worsened this position, even though the Hotz family had a high position in the countryside. The early death of his father in 1751 at the age of 33 made it difficult for the Pestalozzi family to establish itself in the social life of the city: the family simply did not have the financial means. Compared to children of well-situated bourgeois families, Pestalozzi thus grew up in rather reduced circumstances in which frugality was not only a rhetorical virtue but a necessary part of everyday life. The Pestalozzi family was hardly able to benefit from the economic and cultural upswing that Zurich had been experiencing for the last 20 or 30 years, and in the process of the oligarchization of social life it was "on the other side," without ever falling into existential poverty.

Pestalozzi's "school career" was somewhat erratic but eventually continuous and successful. After completing compulsory schooling, which ended at confirmation, Pestalozzi took up his studies at the Zurich Academy in the spring of 1763, which was exactly the time when the republican agitation of the young theology students had experienced a high point with the hasty flight abroad of Grebel, the corrupt bailiff. Apparently fascinated by the study of history under the above-mentioned famous history professor Johann Jacob Bodmer (1698–1783), who had already had an impact on the first "generation" of theologians with revolutionary leanings (see Graber, 1993) and who had assisted his student Vögelin (also mentioned above) in translating Gabriel Bonnot de Mably's (1763) *Entretiens de Phocion*, the young student Pestalozzi became closer to more radical circles, in particular to the "Moral Political and Historical Society."

The Moral Political and Historical Society was founded by ten students in the ages 17 to 22 on July 1, 1762, for the purpose of furthering their education. They were young men who were completing, or had completed, their studies of theology at the Zurich Academy. Their ambition was to acquire political and ethical knowledge and attitudes. Specifically, they aimed to examine the advantages and disadvantages of different forms of government and to study the history of the fatherland. This rather academic goal was elucidated further with an additional important point: on the basis of the academic education, they sought also to form attitudes through which they would become "noble," "patriotic," and "of public usefulness." This comprehensive character education was not to be restricted to their own persons; the young men wanted their body of thought, their vision, to "benefit the entire city state" (Müller, 1762, f.o.8r).

The members themselves were to choose the curriculum for study in the society—that is, they decided what books they wanted to read and discuss. Individual members would give a talk on topics that they chose themselves, and the others would then offer critical comments. The members called themselves "patriots" and "sons of Sparta" (Zehnder-Stadlin, 1875, p. 249), and they were rigid. According to the statutes of the society, the members would hold their discussions "with masculine propriety and instructive seriousness" (Statutes, 1762, Art. 10). Behavior norms for the meetings were laid down accordingly: the drinking of coffee, tea, or wine and the smoking of tobacco were forbidden (Art. 2). Some of the members, whose conduct did not seem serious enough, were even spied upon; it was reported, for example, that some members secretly adjourned to a tavern after the meetings. The report complained, "these indifferent republicans, these supposed followers of the example of Sparta's sons, are slurping down whole bottles of Muscatel and Malvasia..." (as quoted in Zehnder-Stadlin, 1875, p. 249).[1]

In August 1764, after a few months of participating as an auditor at the meetings, Pestalozzi was allowed to take a test for admission to the society as a full member. The test consisted in giving a talk on a topic of his choosing. It would then be critically assessed by the members, who would decide to accept or reject Pestalozzi as a society member. Pestalozzi's presentation, of which Pestalozzi was proud into his old age, paid homage to the Spartan king Agis. It was about the tragic life story of the exemplarily virtuous Spartan king who had tirelessly sacrificed himself to the common good but who, during his absence due to war, was overthrown by a cunning and corrupt tyrant. Through clever comparisons to Demosthenes' speech on the fall of the city of Athens, Pestalozzi was able to draw parallels to the youth movement in Zurich and to the conditions in the city, held to be corrupt, without having to state this directly. The story ends with the triumphal return of Agis to Sparta, made possible by the brave and freedom-loving citizens of Sparta, and with Agis generously pardoning his adversary after he had been sentenced to death. The fallen tyrant, however, subsequently proved to be headstrong and murdered Agis. The moral of the story is quite clear: Tyrants may be—should be, even—killed in the name of the common good (Pestalozzi, 1765/1932).

With this speech, Pestalozzi was not only accepted as a member of the Moral Political and Historical Society but it was also the basis of a "career" in the radical center of the youth movement, which after the dissolution of the society in December 1764 went partly "underground" and prepared targeted actions to radically change the prevailing conditions. The hotheads did not think much of long and drawn out processes of reform. There were plenty of opportunities for public accusations, and the Zurich authorities began increasingly to put aside its originally rather understanding attitude. In the winter of 1766–1767, the authorities proceeded with all severity when the son of a socially underprivileged family (his father was the city trumpeter) wrote a pamphlet publicly criticizing the government of Zurich's decision to send soldiers to Geneva to support the aristocratic little council (*Kleiner Rat*) there against the members of the grand council (*Grosser Rat*), who were demanding more rights (Volz-Tobler, 1997). The author of the pamphlet, Christoph Heinrich Müller (1740–1807), the president of the since dissolved Moral Political and Historical Society, had to flee the city and was only able to return 30 years later. Pestalozzi, who was at first suspected of writing the pamphlet, was interrogated and placed under arrest for three days. Later, for helping Müller to flee, Pestalozzi was fined three stères (cubic meters) of cut wood, which was used by the executioner to burn the "disgraceful" piece in public. On the surface at least, firm intervention by the authorities brought the youth movement to an end. But the young men also began to be interested in topics other than saving the fatherland—namely, in founding a family and choosing an occupation.

3.2 Republican choosing of spouse and occupation

In the five years of the publicly visible youth movement from 1762 to 1767, all of the young theology students who had been active in the patriotic movement had completed their studies, with the exception of Pestalozzi, who had discontinued his studies. All of them were now over 20 years of age and were facing important career and family decisions. Johann Caspar Lavater, who had returned from his educational stay abroad in 1764, married within his social class in 1765; the others were engaged or were at least thinking about starting a family. The requirement for marrying was having an occupation that would provide a family with economic security.

Just how difficult it was for young, radical republican and thus anti-commercial patriots to choose an occupation can be illustrated by Johannes Schulthess (1744–1830), a friend of Pestalozzi's. As the son of a very successful merchant, young Schulthess was to take over his father's business. For a radical republican who saw in commerce the origin of the fall of the city of Zurich, the decision to become a merchant was synonymous with corruption and with contributing to the further decline of the city. In his distress, Schulthess traveled to Val de Travers in 1765, where Jean-Jacques Rousseau (1712–1778) was staying, having sought protection from public persecution after the publication of *Emile* and *The Social Contract*. Val de Travers was a part of the principality of Neuchâtel, which belonged to Prussia at the time and did not join Switzerland until 1815.

Rousseau's recommendation to Schulthess was simple but radical. According to his analysis (and passionate polemics!), it was not only trade that that corrupted people but also at the same time the whole educated world. The only things that one could do, Rousseau advised, was to buy a piece of land far from the city, become a farmer, and to devote oneself humbly and as much as possible to the virtues and to the wellbeing of the fatherland. The ideal in this suggestion was very familiar to Schulthess from the final passages of the fifth volume of Rousseau's *Emile*, published in 1762, in which Sophie and Emile turn to social reform based on agrarian foundations.

Rousseau's plea for the agrarian way of life thus did not fall on unprepared ground, insofar as since the mid-eighteenth century agriculture had entered ever more strongly into the consciousness of many people interested in economics. It was found that agriculture was the indispensable backbone of the economy and that, if reforms were instituted, it could contribute a great deal to the national prosperity. Numerous model farms were established and agricultural theories developed (physiocratic economics, agronomy), and in particular the attempt was made to induce farmers to actually implement technical innovations. In the research literature, the advocates of this agrarian reform movement are called "economic patriots" not without good reason, for increasing agricultural production was seen as increasing the economy of the fatherland, which would benefit everyone, farmers included.

What was radical in Rousseau's proposal was not so much his esteem for agrarian life but rather the circumstance that sons of citizens of the city should themselves live a life in close association with the underprivileged inhabitants of the countryside, especially as the republic of Zurich—in contrast to Bern—traditionally had much closer ties to commerce than to agriculture. The idea inspired by Rousseau of being able to live a modest, virtuous life in nature filled the young radicals of Zurich with enthusiasm, but it was Pestalozzi alone who actually put this plan into practice. He started an agricultural apprenticeship at a model farm in Kirchberg near Burgdorf in the summer of 1767, but he gave it up only 10 months later to buy land near Zurich for his own estate, for which he felt he was sufficiently trained. One of the important reasons for this rather hasty action was his romantic relationship with Anna Schulthess (1738–1815), a self-confident woman of a well-situated and wealthy Zurich bourgeois family, a family that was not pleased with the idea of Pestalozzi as a son-in-law. There were thus obstacles to his courting of Anna, but he was successful. He won her love in 1767, in part through his distressing letters, in which he laid bare his own inadequacies, his love, his unconditional devotion to the fatherland, and promise to give priority to the fatherland over his wife.

In his official proposal to Anna by letter at the beginning of July 1767, Pestalozzi wrote, among other things:

> With regard to marriage, my dear, I must say that I see my duties to my beloved wife as subordinate to my duties to my fatherland and that I, despite the fact that I will be the gentlest of husbands, will still consider it my duty to be merciless towards my wife's tears if she should want to use her tears to keep me from fulfilling my civic duty, no matter what the consequences. (Pestalozzi, 1767/1946, p. 29; freely translated here)

Passages such as this express Pestalozzi's rigorous attitudes, which struck a significant chord with Anna Schulthess and met with her agreement. Her pride in her brave, young, republican suitor, with his (for city terms) underprivileged background and his younger age (8 years younger), turned into love. As her parents were opposed to the relationship with more than skepticism, and because Pestalozzi moved quite far away to the Canton of Bern for his apprenticeship in modern agriculture, Anna and Pestalozzi began a mostly secret correspondence in which their common political ideals became only too apparent and understandable. It is no coincidence that Rousseau played an important role in their letters: "I did not read any part of *Emile* with more attention than I did the story of Sophie," Anna wrote to her beloved Pestalozzi on September 25, 1765 (Schulthess, 1767/1946, p. 117). And if Pestalozzi thought that she would also understand the other four parts of *Emile*, she would do that, too. In the bringing up of their future children, she would of course not be able to contribute to their "physical education" but would instead devote herself mainly to her daughters, who, like the sons, would virtuously abhor the vices. On October 4, 1767, Pestalozzi encouraged his bride-to-be: "Read *Emile*, my Nanette, I know you will understand, and our first piece of business when we meet again will be to read it together" (Pestalozzi, 1767/1946, p. 123).

Pestalozzi and Anna Schulthess were married on September 30, 1769 in the hamlet of Gebenstorf, not far from where Pestalozzi would later build his farmhouse, "Neuhof." Anna's angered parents did not attend the wedding, and they had succeeded in preventing the couple from marrying in the city of Zurich. Soon construction began on Neuhof on land that Pestalozzi had bought near the small village of Birr. Neuhof was not grand, but it still differed from the typical farmhouses of the region. Before they were able move into the farmhouse in the spring of 1771, Anna gave birth to their only child on 14 August 1770, Hans-Jakob (1770–1801), who had epilepsy and due to that a life full of limitations.

3.3 The classical republic of virtue and the opportunities of early industry—Neuhof

In 1767–1768, Pestalozzi learned farming in Kirchberg near Burgdorf as an apprentice to Johann Rudolf Tschiffeli (1716–1780),[2] an economic patriot and secretary of the marriage and morals court of the city of Bern. Pestalozzi's experiences with agriculture and discussion with his teacher very soon relativized his revolutionary republicanism. Here there was no absence of conflicts with friends of his youth in Zurich and especially with his beloved Anna Schulthess—who once accused him of "Paris morals," or untruthfulness. Moreover, Pestalozzi's attitude towards luxury began to change, since he saw that the production of luxury goods, such as embroidery goods, provided farming families with an economic basis. This touched upon a fundamental principle of the republic of virtue—namely, the self-sufficiency of the family household, the *oikos*, which became the center of Pestalozzi's political idealism from this point on.

The ideal of the republic of virtue is the citizen in the sense of *citoyen* (in contrast to *bourgeois*).[3] To best fulfill his roles as head of a family, politician, and soldier, the citizen needs a great deal of economic independence. Since after the mid-1700s farming no longer provided a livelihood for many farming families, Pestalozzi began to see early industry, which in Switzerland developed mainly as cottage industry in the countryside, more and more as a basis of a secure livelihood for families. This meant that he not only had to let go of his strict anti-commercialism, which divided him from the friends of his youth, but also had to distance himself from the "economic patriots," whose national economy concept was based largely on intensified agricultural production.

The issue of securing an economic livelihood of families came to a head in the early 1770s, when catastrophic weather conditions across Europe brought many farmers to subsistence level or below. These conditions were also one of the reasons why Pestalozzi's farm, Neuhof, came into severe difficulties. Everywhere, the numerous private societies created by economic patriots or similar committed contemporaries propagated ways and means to deal with the poverty in the countryside and especially to deal with the children of impoverished families. The "economic patriots" were active in various ways mainly in the two territories of Bern and Zurich. They intensified their attempts of several years' running to teach the rural population improved agricultural methods by means of free instructional literature on topics like fertilization or plowing and popular leaflets showing what plants could be used as food. Other "patriots" published works on the efficient use of small holdings or motivated farmers to combat May beetles and sparrows, which threatened the harvest. They also called for free school meals, and tried to get farmers to plant potatoes, which had been newly introduced in Switzerland, and bake potato bread.

Pestalozzi evidently sought another route. In the early 1770s he had already begun to expand his agricultural enterprise to include early industrial production—mainly weaving and spinning. In the face of enormous financial strain and the failed harvests, he found himself forced to gradually replace the adult workers in his weaving operation with the cheaper labor of children. He promised poor families that he would give their children a good education, the cost of which could be paid for by their own labor working part-time in the production of early industrial goods. On this basis, many farming families that had fallen on hard times sent their children to Neuhof. This enterprise, with a factory room and a children's house, was at first looked on very favorably. Pestalozzi sent out and published begging letters several times and received private monies in support of his philanthropic work, and he also received money from Bern, to which Neuhof belonged. But when after a few years, despite Pestalozzi's promises, the aimed-for financial security of the operation did not come about, public support for Neuhof dropped significantly. Neuhof would have become bankrupt in 1799 if Pestalozzi's father-in-law, Hans Jacob Schulthess (1711–1789), had not paid off all debts under the condition that Pestalozzi henceforth seek other means of employment.

3.4 Agriculture with or without early industry?

In the mid-1770s Pestalozzi's institute at Neuhof had become known through his public announcements and through reports in magazines. He achieved the status of a credible reformer shortly thereafter, when he became involved in a public debate on the foundations and strategies of education of the rural poor. This debate took place in a periodical that aimed to bring together the reform discussion in France, England, the United States, Germany, and Switzerland. The editor of the journal, *Ephemeriden der Menschheit*,[4] was Isaak Iselin (1728–1782), council secretary of the city of Basel, who also published in the journal his own essay, *Schreiben eines Vaters an seinen Sohn, der sich der Handelschaft widmet* [Letter of a Father to His Son Who is Devoted to Trade] (Iselin, 1781) described above.

Pestalozzi's opponent in the debate was Niklaus Emanuel von Tscharner (1727–1794), a patrician of Bern and one of the most prominent "economic patriots." At the very time that Pestalozzi bought Neuhof (1769–1770), Tscharner was serving only five kilometers away as a magistrate (from 1767 to 1773) in the government office of Schenkenburg. Due to Tscharner's excellent reputation as an agronomist, Iselin asked him to write an article on the education of poor rural children for the first issue of the new periodical (Tscharner, 1776–1777).

Tscharner's reflections on the topic were published in various issues of *Ephemeriden* in 1776 and 1777 in the form of 17 letters. This was precisely the time when Pestalozzi was developing his work/education institute for the poor at Neuhof. Tscharner's letters contain no coherent (social) pedagogical concept and do not express any doubts concerning the political and social structure of Bern. The content is occasionally repetitious, and Tscharner sometimes even contradicts himself. It is especially interesting that whereas Tscharner was familiar with Pestalozzi's institute for poor children and even supported it financially, he did not mention it even once in any of the 17 letters. Tscharner held to a dual notion of education, divided into moral education, which is general and for all social classes, and physical education, which had to be class-oriented, meaning that it had to prepare a person for an occupation. The aim of education was for each person to be happy in the station to which he had been born, which meant that everyone had to be convinced of the dignity of their own station. In terms of organization, Tscharner had in mind a state-supported institution with a wealthy benefactor who fulfills his philanthropic life's work and to whom all children show thanks and humility.

When Tscharner's twelfth letter was published in November 1776, Pestalozzi responded in the form of personal letters to him, who—given his domestic proximity to Neuhof—can be considered Pestalozzi's neighbor. In the letters he discussed his *practical* experience with the education of the poor children at Neuhof, which bore no witness to benefactors, state support, or humble, thankful children. There is no record of Tscharner's immediate reaction to Pestalozzi's account from an opposing point of view, but he did send Pestalozzi's letters to his editor in Basel, Iselin, who then published them in *Ephemeriden*, too (Pestalozzi, 1777/1932).

In the letters, which became known as Pestalozzi's Neuhof writings, Pestalozzi joins together two aims: first, public legitimization of his institute for the poor and thus further financial support, and second, propagation of an institute for the poor based on early industry. This latter aim positioned him ideologically in opposition to not only his former radical patriot friends but also the agrarian patriots in Bern and Zurich. Paradoxically, early industry seemed to Pestalozzi to be the only way to allow the idea of the republic of virtue to rise again. The issue in the foreground was not the corruptibility of the city souls of the factory owners and merchants but rather the circumstance that no virtue could be expected of anyone if they had no secure livelihood. Pestalozzi had expanded the narrow circle of the republic limited to the city to the rural countryside, not to sue for political participation of the rural population but instead to foster public virtue on the basis of economic security. For this, two conditions had to be met: first, country people needed an education that taught them to handle the new way of life and handle money without succumbing to the dangers involved, and second, the economic laws had to be liberalized such that the countryside would no longer be massively disadvantaged vis-à-vis the city. In other words, what was required was fundamental political reform of the Swiss city-states.

Notes

1. For a more detailed account of the history of this society based on archival materials, see Tröhler (2009).
2. http://en.wikipedia.org/wiki/Johann_Rudolf_Tschiffeli
3. The polemic opposition between *citoyen* and *bourgeois* goes back to Rousseau and indicates the contradiction between a person oriented towards the common good and the selfish inhabitant of a city or a state.

4 *Ephemeriden der Menschheit* was modeled after the French periodical *Ephémérides du citoyen ou chronique de l'esprit national*, which was edited from 1765 to 1772 by French economist Nicolas Baudeau (http://en.wikipedia.org/wiki/Nicolas_Baudeau) and which can be viewed as the mouthpiece of the French physiocrats.

4
The Christian Republic, Enlightenment, and Coercive Education

Abstract: Pestalozzi's experiment in becoming a farmer failed due to several different reasons. Though his integrating of poor children in the farm, trading their cheap labor for basic education, Pestalozzi became some sort of an expert in education. In a peculiar entanglement of his personal fate with that of the rural population, he began to stand up for political reform that basically aimed at giving the rural population more economic freedom, so that families could become more independent, which had always been a prerequisite of classical republicanism: persons that have to be concerned with their economic welfare cannot be guided by the common good, and this holds for both the greedy wealthy and for the very poor. The need for reform was recognized; however, in contrast to his classical-republican ideals in Zurich Pestalozzi's concrete political objectives for the rural population were now for a Christian republic under the direction of an outstanding politician (selfless and dedicated to common welfare)—a kind of mythical "first legislator" along the lines of Lycurgus, the legendary lawgiver of Sparta, who had become known from Rousseau's Social Contract.

Tröhler, Daniel. *Pestalozzi and the Educationalization of the World*. New York: Palgrave Macmillan, 2013.
DOI: 10.1057/9781137346858.

Around 1780 Pestalozzi, 34 years old, was known in Switzerland as an educator of the poor, but occupationally he was ruined. He remained at Neuhof until the outbreak of the Helvetic Revolution in 1798 and was in principle unemployed, first making some money by his publications and later, after 1790, by helping, as a citizen of Zurich, entrepreneurs of the underprivileged Zurich countryside to do their commerce. In a peculiar entanglement of his personal fate with that of the rural population, he began to stand up for political reform that basically aimed at giving the rural population more economic freedom so that families could become more independent, which had always been a prerequisite of classical republicanism: persons who have to be concerned with their economic welfare cannot be guided by the common good, and this holds for both the greedy wealthy and for the very poor. The need for reform was recognized; however, the concrete political objectives for the rural population were rather for a Christian republic[1] under the direction of an outstanding politician (selfless and dedicated to common welfare). The idea of a mythical "first legislator" goes back to Lycurgus, the legendary lawgiver of Sparta[2] and had been reactivated in Rousseau's *Social Contract*:

> The legislator is in all respects an extraordinary man in the State. If he ought to be so by his genius, he is not less so by his office. It is neither magistracy nor sovereignty. This office, which constitutes the republic, does not enter into its constitution; it is a special and superior office, having nothing in common with human jurisdictions. (Rousseau 1762/2002, p. 181)

Along with this tradition of praising "first legislators," Pestalozzi conceptualized a literary character who was at once a lawgiver, powerful authority, and judge: Carl Arner, the county bailiff in the novel *Leonard and Gertrude* (1781ff.).

4.1 Political reforms and the Christian republic of *Lienhard und Gertrud* (1781)

The oligarchization of the Swiss city-states in the eighteenth century had been made possible among other things by the increasing discrimination against the rural population. At the level of the territory as a whole, the rural population had never had any political say, and rural inhabitants had had very little chance of military careers. But specific legislation in the eighteenth century additionally disadvantaged the rural population as opposed to the city inhabitants. The city dwellers had decided for an extensive trade monopoly, which forced the rural homeworkers not only to buy raw materials exclusively from city merchants but also to sell their finished products to city citizens only. This economic policy aiming at advantage for the city dwellers prevented better and more lasting economic growth in the countryside—growth which could have benefitted many of the poor, particularly those who did not own land.

The possibility of a partial economic reorientation of the republic on the basis of early industry thus demanded economic policy reform—that is, liberalization of the economic laws that had granted such massive privilege to city citizens. To this purpose, Pestalozzi wrote an essay in 1779 that was not by chance titled *Von der Freyheit meiner Vaterstatt!* [On the Freedom of the Father City!] (Pestalozzi, 1779/1932). The term freedom points to the heart of republicanism—namely, the freedom of the people to draft their own laws, a privilege, from which the countryside was obviously excluded. But—probably because of censorship—this political participation was not the subject of Pestalozzi's reflections. He focused instead on the rural population's lack of sufficient economic freedom—that is, their denied right to acquire economic *Wohlstand* [welfare, prosperity] and thus to support the family and on this basis to lead secure and virtuous lives.

According to Pestalozzi, this unfortunate situation had been caused by the (selfish) citizens of the city of Zurich, who had made improper use of their political freedom, abusing it to gain economic advantages over the rural population. The political and economic freedom of the citizens required something that the citizens of Zurich evidently no longer possessed—namely, *Freiheitssinn*, the moral freedom or moral strength of the individual to be satisfied with prosperity and not strive after great wealth. Apparently it was precisely this inner moral strength that the city citizens lacked. The sudden wealth that had become possible in Zurich with commerce and cottage industry after 1700 had made the nouveau riche so dizzy that they had created legal privileges for themselves that had brought them even more riches, instead of seeing to it that the whole population could benefit from the wealth. Not only was the countryside massively disadvantaged, but also the money had led to alienation on the part of the city citizens. In Pestalozzi's opinion, in the preceding decades power holders of the city republic of Zurich had come into the top positions suspending for selfish reasons the very basis of the republic (which was prosperity for all) and had thus rung in the decline of the republic. Not the poor but the rich were to blame for the decline of the republic: "The socially disadvantaged inhabitant is not the cause of the national corruption; he suffers in moral and economic hardship from the corruption that comes from above, the source of which is to be found in the inner undermining of our constitution" (Pestalozzi, 1779/1932, p. 238; freely translated here).

Corrupt magistrates used their power to increase their own wealth and in this way let the republic down. In the cycle of wealth and corruption that Pestalozzi diagnosed, there was no outlook for liberalization that would benefit the rural population. Pestalozzi saw no other way out than to emphasize the ideal of a Christian magistrate or a Christian version of the "first legislator"—an ideal going back to pre-Christian Antiquity. The Christian ideal Pestalozzi was referring to now had been characterized strikingly by the Zurich reformer Huldrych Zwingli (1484–1531),[3] whose writings Pestalozzi was familiar with from his studies: noble and generous, strong, selfless, always examining himself, guided by consideration of the common welfare. In other words, the ideas of the classical republic of virtues would from now on live on in the Christian republic. In a few short weeks in 1779–1780, Pestalozzi wrote on his notions of what that kind of life could be and how corrupt conditions were to be dealt with. Iselin, council secretary of Basel, took on Pestalozzi's manuscript, spent a long time correcting it in style and grammar, and saw to it that the work was published as a novel, *Lienhard und Gertrud*, in 1781.[4]

Lienhard und Gertrud, or *Leonard and Gertrude*, as it is titled in English, tells the story of a husband and wife in the village of Bonnal, which due to poor higher government is being increasingly dominated by a power- and money-greedy "upper class." Leonard, a mason, is a kind man, but he is not immune to temptation, and he owes money to Hummel, who is both the village bailiff and proprietor of a tavern. Threatening Leonard with the law, Hummel forces Leonard to continue drinking at his beer-house, which only increases his debts and brings his family to the brink of ruin. The opposite of Leonhard is personified by his wife, Gertrude, a religious and strong character who despite their dire financial straits feeds and clothes the family thanks to her iron discipline. Once Leonard has explained his debts and Hummel's power over him to Gertrude, she gathers up all her courage as well as her meager savings and goes to see

Arner, the district bailiff (upper magistrate). She bemoans her fate in a corrupt village. At the same time, she asks Arner for advice on how their remaining money could pay off Leonard's debts. Arner, without doubt a character based by Pestalozzi on Niklaus Emanuel Tscharner, subsequently institutes a number of political and economic reforms that sets boundaries on the behavior of the "village aristocracy" and makes it possible for the craftsmen to work and earn money. Within a short time, so it seems, a village full of injustices is turned into a little paradise, thanks to a virtuous, selfless, district bailiff who is always—in the manner of a good Protestant—willing to examine himself. The readership of *Lienhard und Gertrud* seems to have been extremely touched by this communal vision, not least due to the description of the ideal magistrate.

However, the fact that Pestalozzi published further parts of the novel in 1783, 1785, and 1787 that had not been planned at all and that went in a different direction shows that basing the political ideal on the Christian-republican magistrate was not a solution that Pestalozzi found convincing for long, for the reason alone that no such magistrates existed.

4.2 The disillusionment of the Swiss republics

The novel *Lienhard und Gertrud* (1781) met with great success. This seemed to buoy Pestalozzi up, who had become an increasingly isolated "dropout" from Zurich society and who was worn down by the de facto bankruptcy of Neuhof (in 1779). However, the death of his mentor Iselin in 1782 put a terrible damper on things. In addition, real domestic policy developments in the Swiss territories did not go in the direction of Pestalozzi's political objectives. In reality there were no upper authorities like Arner to be seen, and the cities of the Swiss city-states made no move to change their economic policies supporting their own interests. Therefore, conditions in the countryside would not come to resemble Pestalozzi's depiction of a simple republic of virtue where people would have sufficient security to be able to develop virtuously. Pestalozzi's political disappointment was combined with a feeling of personal insult in connection with the closing of Neuhof, which—and this he believed to the end of his days—could have been avoided if the government had given him enough support.

Already when he wrote the first two volumes of *Lienhard und Gertrud* in 1780 and 1781 (the second volume was not published until 1783), Pestalozzi was beginning to place his hopes in a real "super magistrate," specifically Emperor Joseph II[5] (1741–1790) of Austria, who had become ruler of the Hapsburg lands in 1780 upon the death of his mother, Empress Maria Theresa[6] (1717–1780), who had instituted comprehensive reforms along the lines of enlightened absolutism. Seeing Iselin's lodge brother-type relations with officials at the court of Vienna, Pestalozzi hoped for employment at the emperor's court as a kind of Swiss Voltaire (Voltaire had been in Potsdam with a similar "mission"). He wanted to be a writer/philosopher who would serve as an intermediary between the government and the people on national reform, and he wanted to establish a new institute for the poor with state funding. To that purpose he wrote some short plays, which appeared in 1782 in a weekly journal, *Ein Schweizer-Blatt*, that Pestalozzi himself published for the period of one year. As to their literary quality, the short plays were on the same level as *Lienhard und Gertrud* but they were not nearly as widely received. He also wrote tracts on reforming social and criminal laws, which he sent to Iselin with the request that Iselin forward them to appropriate persons at the court of Vienna, so that he would become known to them and be invited to court. He also joined the Order of the Illuminati, of which Iselin and many other Swiss were members and which was also well represented at the emperor's court.

Pestalozzi's attempts to obtain employment in Vienna were in vain, however. Iselin died in 1782, leaving Pestalozzi without his good connection to the Austrian capital. The only contact that Iselin had made for Pestalozzi, by sending the first volume of *Lienhard und Gertrud* to Karl Johann Christian von Zinzendorf (1739–1813), a senior civil servant, was maintained. But it was mainly Pestalozzi who kept up communications, by sending tracts and further parts of *Lienhard und Gertrud*. The recipients were not uninterested, but the relationships never led to employment in Vienna, particularly as Count Zinzendorf, who was himself very familiar with the discussion on reform in Europe, and did not at all have the kind of responsibility that would make it possible for him to induce the emperor to hire a Swiss. In his letters Pestalozzi quite skillfully tried to cover up his republican origins by name dropping and presenting himself as a part of the Swiss reform aristocracy. When he sent Zinzendorf the fourth volume of *Lienhard und Gertrud* on May 26,

1787, he referred in his letter to Daniel von Fellenberg (1736–1801), an aristocrat in Bern, and stated that lasting reforms in Europe could be expected only from Austria:

> Fellenberg himself wrote to me: "From our corrupt republic I have no hopes of advancement for the people." It is humiliating for us, but true: the advance of true leadership of the people must be prepared in the cabinets of wise princes; from us this progress will definitely not ensue—we are done. (Pestalozzi, 1787/1949, p. 246)

Paradoxically, in Pestalozzi's despair he did not see hope for the revival of the republic in the republics themselves, which seemed irreversibly corrupt, but rather in a monarchy that was reform-oriented thanks to a magistrate at the highest level.

4.3 The popular Enlightenment and modern natural law

Like most Swiss publicists of the eighteenth century, Pestalozzi saw himself not as a literary author but as a political author, which also motivated him at times to criticize Goethe and other German authors who, in his opinion, did not put their writing genius to sufficient use in the cause of comprehensive social reform. For Pestalozzi, writing was an aesthetic means to an end: political and social reform. Upon this background, he began in 1782 to concern himself with a discussion that had not played an important role in either the youth movement in Zurich or in economic patriotism—namely, the Enlightenment literature (primarily in Berlin). Of main importance here was the journal *Berliner Monatsschrift*, published by German jurist and philosopher Johann Erich Biester (1749–1816) starting in 1783. Pestalozzi's incredibly long excerpts from the journal show the topics that were increasingly capturing his attention: they were issues of social justice, property, (vocational) education and training, and—over time more and more—the anthropological question of the nature of man and thus the foundations of human society. As for most Swiss, for Pestalozzi man—particularly republican man—was a *zoon politikon*, or political being by nature, a being who can find full development only in the *polis*.

However, the modern European discussion in natural law had long questioned that assumption, as it assumed that man was originally not a political but a pre-social being. The idea was that man lived together with other human beings only because he had made a contract with them, a social contract. But that meant that "by nature" all people were to be seen as the same, and as contractual partners they were allowed to interact on an equal footing. The politically explosive force of this thinking after the mid-eighteenth century—the high point of absolutism in Europe—cannot be underestimated, as the notion of an originally just social contract between equal partners could be used very easily for criticism of the existing political conditions, as Jean-Jacques Rousseau (1712–1778) had shown brilliantly in his famous prize essay, *Discours sur l'origine et les fondements de l'inégalité parmi les hommes* [Discourse on the Origin and the Foundations of Inequality among Men] (Rousseau, 1755).

The idea of human beings as originally pre-social beings led Pestalozzi to numerous revisions of his political conception of man. He did not give up his original republican ideal, but he sought new ways, on the basis of a different conception of man, to come as close as possible to achieving the ideals of the republic of virtues. Two elements emerged out of his study of the Enlightenment literature in the 1780s: first, man is a being concerned with his welfare and, on this basis, in his dealings with others he develops egoism. This being finds in possession and property, a means to ease his worry about his welfare. However, to keep his property secure, he must make special efforts to protect it. And because other people also need secure property, they conclude a contract among themselves that assures each the safety of his property. Thus, *property* becomes the foundation of human society, not a vision of freedom of some type or other. Secured ownership of property, according to Pestalozzi, brought human beings not only rights (the right to secure property) but also obligations.

The canon of republican virtues that Pestalozzi had formerly called "natural" now became social obligations between human beings—parents and children, magistrates and subjects, rich and poor. Delinquent poor who steal out of hunger and become otherwise brutalized are not only evil criminals but victims of unjust distribution of goods and the failure of the authorities to fulfill their obligation—and that held also for young, unmarried women who commit infanticide.[7] Pestalozzi's aim here was not an egalitarian society but rather a society in which secure property guarantees "independence," an alternate term for freedom. It was the task of the law to secure property and to keep people under control. And it was the task of (class-oriented) vocational education to enable people to take care of their property and to check their originally acquired brutality and roughness in their dealings with other people. In a clear rejection of the Zwinglian republic and thus of *Lienhard und Gertrud* (1781), Pestalozzi now banned morality and religion from the realm of the state. Besides the laws and education, social regulation consisted only in handed-down customs and standards. The latter should keep social interactions civil and make sure that man's original lack of restraint and his egoism would be held in check. The system of laws and customs was not moral, affecting the inward position of the humans, but was merely the fence keeping the animal in man from running riot (Pestalozzi, 1783/1930, p. 214).

4.4   *Lienhard und Gertrud*, parts 3 and 4 (1785 and 1787)

Traces of the two developments in the 1780s—Pestalozzi's turn to enlightened absolutism and to Enlightenment literature—can be found in the unplanned further volumes of *Lienhard und Gertrud*, mainly in the last two, published in 1785 and 1787. The turn to the natural law discussion, or the anthropology of modern natural law, is visible in volume three of *Lienhard und Gertrud* (Pestalozzi, 1785/1928), of all things in connection with the introduction of the village school master. This teacher, a long-serving and worldly wise lieutenant, is named Glüphi, which suggests that Pestalozzi is making him his mouthpiece as GLÜPHI could be the anagram of the first letters of *Johann Heinrich Pestalozzi über Lienhard (und) Gertrud* [Johann Heinrich Pestalozzi about Leonard (and) Gertrude]. But whatever the explanation of this strange name, it is the village school master that along with the district bailiff Carl Arner becomes responsible for extensive reform, together with Baumwoll-Meyer ("Cotton" Meyer), a man with a lot of moral integrity whose great success as a cotton processor and merchant had not corrupted him. Like the character of Arner, Cotton Meyer was based on a real person in Pestalozzi's neighborhood—namely, Johann Rudolf Meyer (1739–1813), a regional silk ribbon manufacturer.

Over the last two parts of the novel, Arner himself becomes more and more unimportant in a certain sense. It suddenly becomes apparent that he is not a citizen of a republican city-state at all, and as such is serving in the office of upper magistrate/governor, which was without doubt in part one of the novel (Pestalozzi, 1781); instead he is an official from a court quite some distance away. This is a clear indication of how little Pestalozzi now expected of the Swiss republics. Arner receives a letter from a certain Count Bylifsky, a character who is generally believed to represent the real Count Zinzendorf. Bylifsky is a reform-oriented civil servant at the court, where there are evil doings underway to undermine Arner's reform program in the village of Bonnal, among other things. Arner falls ill under all the pressures and is on his deathbed. He survives, but his illness had made him see that too many of the bases of the village's fortune are connected to his person—that is, to his moral integrity as a person. Shaken by the continuing attacks of corrupt stakeholders at the court and by his own weak condition, Arner decides to guarantee the people's rights in writing, so that their rights will be secured also in times under "bad" authorities. The good, Christian magistrate as a model has thus been retired, and the safeguard of legal guarantees has taken its place. The legal world was not to replace the authority of a morally purified magistrate but to act as safeguard if a magistrate should turn out to be more selfish than morally purified.

Just how urgently especially underprivileged people like the inhabitants of the village Bonnal needed this legal protection is shown clearly by Glüphi's anthropology and educational concept. In Pestalozzi's unusually strong language, man is described as a wild animal that must be held in check by all means or he will do all he can to exploit others. Pestalozzi's evident rancor about man's egoistic nature finds clear expression in a chapter in volume four of *Lienhard und Gertrud* (Pestalozzi, 1787/1928), titled "Die Philosophie meines Leutnants und diejenige meines Buchs" [The Philosophy of My Lieutenant and of My Book]: by nature man is, when left to grow up wild, lazy, ignorant, rash, unwary, imprudent, gullible, fearful, and greedy beyond all measure, and if he meets with obstacles to satisfying his needs, he becomes dishonest, devious, malicious, mistrustful, violent, bold, vengeful, and cruel. This view of man demands of prudent "*Menschenführung*" [leadership] such that it must turn man into something very different than what man is by nature, so that he does not injure society and his fellow men. In other words, man has to be made socially suitable in the first place by means of institutions, moral customs and standards, ways of educating, and laws, which change him on the inside and win him around (Pestalozzi, 1787/1928, pp. 330f.).

The Bonnal village school that Glüphi sets up is not intended to provide empty verbal instruction but instead primarily to provide comprehensive vocational training. As the young people in the village would later be either farmers or textile (cotton) workers, they were to learn as much as needed to be able to do their work properly. Educating through love alone was rejected, because people must learn to later root out thorns and thistles, as Pestalozzi put it in the words of Glüphi and in reference to Genesis 3:18. The natural egoism of social man had to be eradicated, so that the purpose of society, independence through property, could be achieved: whoever wanted to achieve something with people or wanted to make something of them, the school master said, had to overcome their malice, pursue their falseness, and drive out the cold sweat of them on their crooked ways (Pestalozzi, 1785/1928, p. 173). The republic, which consists of inhabitants who have become independent through sufficient prosperity and thus have become virtuous, requires iron leadership that keeps the originally asocial nature of man in strict check through education, laws, and moral standards.

It is certainly impressive how Pestalozzi attempted, shortly before the French Revolution, to rescue the ideal of the republic of virtue through a relatively rigid educational and political regime that is intended to first of all make people "good," before they can make ethical use of freedom. With this—for a start limited to literary fiction—Pestalozzi took a big step in the direction of an educational turn. However, the French Revolution would soon begin and delay this turn somewhat.

Notes

1. Instead of the republic of virtue, which was intended for the educated city citizens.
2. http://en.wikipedia.org/wiki/Lycurgus_of_Sparta
3. http://en.wikipedia.org/wiki/Huldrych_Zwingli
4. A French translation was published in 1783: *Léonard et Gertrude: ou les moeurs villageoise* (Pestalozzi, 1783). This French translation was the basis for the first English translation, which was published in 1800 under the title *Leonard & Gertrude: A popular story, written originally in German; translated into French, and now attempted in English; with the hope of its being useful to the lower orders of society* (Pestalozzi, 1800). A first American translation was published under the same title in Philadelphia in 1801 (Pestalozzi, 1801).
5. http://en.wikipedia.org/wiki/Joseph_II,_Holy_Roman_Emperor

6 http://en.wikipedia.org/wiki/Maria_Theresa
7 The discussion on how young women who committed infanticide should be dealt with was one of the very big issues in the late eighteenth century. The discussion focused on young, unmarried women who became pregnant, were abandoned by men, and killed their infants out of desperation. In 1780 a public essay competition was held in Germany on the best way to solve this problem. The announcement of the competition unleashed a flood of essays on the topic, of which not all of them were sent in for judging—among them an essay by Pestalozzi titled *Über Gesetzgebung und Kindermord* [On legislation and infanticide] (Pestalozzi, 1783). In the research literature, Pestalozzi's response is considered to be the most fully developed analysis of the problem; it shifts the view from the perpetrator, the woman committing infanticide, to the unjust laws that fostered infanticide. Pestalozzi called for the abolishment of a law that prohibited marriage for the very poor, which in fact amounted to prohibition of sexual intercourse, and demanded criminal prosecution of men who impregnate women and desert them, the establishment of state homes for unmarried women to give birth, and state protection of unmarried mothers.

5
The American and the French Republics, German Idealism, and the Principle of Inwardness

Abstract: *In the 12 years between the ratification of the first constitution of the United States and the Reign of Terror in France 1793 to July 1794, Pestalozzi wrestled with the issue of the best possible political constitution for the political community. To Pestalozzi, the Swiss republics seemed to be in a hopelessly corrupt state, so at first he saw enlightened absolutism as the means to guarantee the foundations of classical republicanism: secure livelihood and thus the appropriate level of prosperity—not riches!—that allows people to devote themselves to the common good. Just how the right to private property should be reconciled with the duty to the common good was the central question of those 12 years. He would not find his (preliminary) "answer" in either the American or in the French Republic and certainly not in the context of the old Swiss republics but rather, of all things, in German idealism, which was strongly indebted to Lutheran Protestantism.*

Tröhler, Daniel. *Pestalozzi and the Educationalization of the World.* New York: Palgrave Macmillan, 2013.
DOI: 10.1057/9781137346858.

Between the ratification of the first constitution of the United States in 1781, and the Reign of Terror in France from September 1793 to July 1794, Pestalozzi wrestled the question of the best possible political order. Disappointed by the Swiss republics and disenchanted by the French developments Pestalozzi sought a solution within German idealism. The "answer," which Pestalozzi developed from 1793 to 1797, assumed that in the innermost being of all persons there was a unique power with which they can even out the fundamental tension between the right of ownership and social constraints. Strengthening this power was essentially an educational task, for which there were two strategies: early and extensive education in the family home based on love and, somewhat later, accommodation to order and discipline based on schooling and vocational education and training.

5.1 Freedom, property, and social obligations

In 1781 Pestalozzi published his successful novel, *Lienhard und Gertrud*, and immediately set about writing a second volume, which was published in 1783. In the interim he also published short dramas dealing with moral and political topics in the weekly magazine, *Ein Schweizer-Blatt*, of which he himself was the publisher. The (republican) permanent topic was how freedom and property could be guaranteed without fostering corruption. Pestalozzi had come to the conclusion that a "good" monarchy was preferable to a "bad" republic when it came to the actual goal of a republic—namely, public virtue. Good government, no matter what the political system, must be able to distribute privileges justly, so that all people could benefit from them. A short dramatic scene written by Pestalozzi (1782/1927a) will serve to illustrate this; titled *Scenen im Innern Frankreichs, nach der Natur gezeichnet* [Naturalistic Scenes in France], it was published by Pestalozzi in *Schweizer-Blatt*. It made a connection between corrupted monarchy and selfish aristocracy and interpreted the American independence from the point of view of this monarchical-aristocratic corruption.

The events in America were being widely discussed in Europe, and they met with approval mainly in republican settings. Johann Rodolph de Valltravers, a scientist in Bern who had been in correspondence with Benjamin Franklin since the 1760s, wrote to Franklin in this connection on April 14, 1778:

> Since both Commonwealths, your and our XIII. united Cantons, are become the faithfull Allies of France, what should hinder us, to form between us

both, such a Connection of Amity, of acknowledging and warranting our Independence, of mutual Defense against all Invaders, and of reciprocal good offices, as Might still add to our Security, and avert any sinister Designs of ambitious Neighbours upon our Liberties?...Let us be united, as two Sister-Republicks, in spite of all arbitrary, invidious, and infesting Ennemies! (as quoted in Willcox, 1987, p. 293)

The Swiss public and thus also Pestalozzi were familiar with the Declaration of Independence of the 13 United States of America through diverse publications in Iselin's *Ephemeriden*. In the very first issue of *Ephemeriden* in January 1776, Iselin had reported optimistically on the *Neue Interimsrepublic* [new temporary republic] (Neue Interimsrepublic, 1776), and in October of the same year he printed the first and only complete German translation of the Declaration of Independence, which was signed by the president of the Continental Congress, John Hancock (Englische Kolonien in Amerika, 1776). In 1777 Iselin printed the texts of the first constitution of the 13 United States, the Articles of Confederation (Bündnis der vereinigten Staaten in America, 1777) and also the constitutions of the State of Pennsylvania and State of Delaware (Entwurf der pensylvanischen Regierungsform, 1777; Pensylvanische Regierungsform, 1777; Grundsätze, 1777).

Pestalozzi's *Scenen im Innern Frankreichs* show very clearly how the question of the political order was only measured against the criterion of whether it was possible for all persons to gain sufficient prosperity so as to be able to fulfill their social responsibility, and it shows very clearly that extreme unequal distribution of power involves the extreme unequal distribution of prosperity, leading to extreme wealth and extreme poverty. It is also an impressive illustration of how a formal system—a constitutional republic—could be infiltrated from above by corruption.

Pestalozzi's dramatic scene is set in a French country castle. Four persons are amusing themselves by playing a game of cards: a count, an abbot, a marquess, and a young noblewoman. Their topics of conversation are commerce, bourgeoisie, and political events. Regarding the French support of the American soldiers in the war against England, they praise "free America" and in particular France's achievements. "Our victory is a tribute to man—we are saving half the world from slavery," says the abbot (Pestalozzi, 1782/1927a, p. 24; freely translated here), while the marquess boasts, "our Enlightenment opened up the decade for freedom and humanity." The count confirms that freedom is on everyone's lips, whereby the marquess reminds them that with this reform, the aristocracy has to see carefully to their priority and see to it that the sources of money connected with freedom do not fall into the hands of commoners. The count reassures everyone, remarking that through targeted corrupting of the common citizens—such as occasionally giving them admittance to balls, and for their money opening up to them the antichambers, comedy houses, and amusement parks—common man would soon himself cause sufficient damage to himself. The abbot concurs with the marquess' conclusion that freedom would apparently be good for them by saying: "It raises and refines the comforts and advantages in the upper classes immeasurably: Meanwhile, the lower classes, in their freedom and with unbelievable arduousness, bring us the funds for this increased enjoyment of life, and call themselves blessed to be allowed to do so" (p. 24f.).

The marquess then tells them of his plan to build factories in America, as soon as it declares free trade, since the farmers on his country estates are practically "croaking" and are unable to bring him in enough money (Pestalozzi, 1782/1927a, p. 25f.). This conversation is then interrupted by the young noblewoman, who has spotted through the window a horrible scene in the inner courtyard of the castle—namely, a mother with her nine children eating the dogs' food out of desperate hunger. She has come to the castle to obtain the release of her husband, who has been locked up for poaching. The noble group turns away from the sight indignantly, saying that unfortunately one was faced with such scenes in the countryside, and discussing how the room could be rebuilt to prevent views of the courtyard. The estate manager, whose job it is to make sure that all is in order, brings the group a note from the pastor requesting that the family man be pardoned. Their discussion about the pastor and the farmers exposes the men to be inhumane, decadent, corrupt, and they are for this reason unwilling to secure for farmers even basic income and basic rights. At the end of the scene, they resume their game of cards and their contemptuous and disdaining conversation about the people, which expresses Pestalozzi's rancor against corrupt regents and their disastrous social consequences (p. 29f.). For both extremes, very great wealth and very great poverty, are corrupting—that is, both wealth and poverty distract people from their social duties.

The solution can be found in only one direction—namely, in the development of a certain kind of strength that Pestalozzi called the "strength to overcome," people's strength to overcome their own egoism. Basically, the building of this virtue was meant for farmers as well as for "the lordships." No household, whether the family in the case of the farmer or the land in the case of the regent, was to be set up according to the personal desires and whims of the man responsible. Instead, those in power must always act in a way appropriate to their power and their goods, and "in this circumstance lies the true fundament of the education of the nobleman, which is so very important for the farmers and for humanity; he must be educated, in the head and the heart, for the circle of his sovereignty" (Pestalozzi, 1782/1927c, p. 63). And the farmer must be—and here we find a typical expression of the educationalization of social problems—specially educated, because with the coming proto-industry he will come into cash money and will thus be ever more strongly tempted to lead an imprudent way of life, in particular to imitate the lifestyle of the rich. The new factory earnings—money—create two major dangers, "miserliness, theft, and fraud" and "slovenliness and wastefulness," and "avoiding both of them requires special care for domestic enlightenment and good manners," to which people had to be educated (Pestalozzi, 1782/1927b, p. 55).

5.2 The French Revolution and Pestalozzi's position

Although the Storming of the (ramshackle) Bastilles on July 14, 1789 is a symbol of the French Revolution, the revolution had begun much earlier and had not ended with the taking of the prison. The reception of the event on the European and North American continents was also quite gradual. Whereas the events at the very beginning had received great attention and had lured numerous onlookers to Paris, including Wilhelm von Humboldt (1767–1835),[1] who was drawn to Paris along with his mentor, Johann Joachim Heinrich Campe[2] (1746–1818). However, it took a while before judgments had been formed on the Revolution, and over time they began to diverge more and more, because they had increasing domestic political explosiveness. At first, as an event in the great French monarchy, the Revolution had been met with interest and even amusement, but it soon became relevant for the other nations themselves. Particularly when it became clear in 1792 that after the power takeover by the Jacobins and the *sans-culottes* the setting up of a constitutional monarchy had failed and that a democratic republic was to be established through the Reign of Terror, skepticism and disapproval began to predominate abroad. This was reinforced by the execution of King Louis XVI and Queen Marie Antoinette in 1793. After these events, people who still spoke in favor of the developments in France were usually viewed with distrust, especially by persons in positions of power. This was also and especially true for Pestalozzi, who in August 1792—to his complete surprise—was awarded honorary French citizenship by the French parliament along with 16 other famous foreign persons, including three Founding Fathers of the United States, George Washington, Alexander Hamilton, and James Madison.[3] This was just at the time when the revolutionaries stormed the Tuileries Palace and shortly before the September Massacres. This great recognition of Pestalozzi, who in Switzerland was socially isolated, came for him at a most inopportune moment, for in the storming of the Tuileries Palace the French revolutionists had killed the Swiss Guards protecting the French king.

Pestalozzi had been interested in the abolishment of the French monarchy and the establishment of a republic, but in 1793 to 1794 he condemned the excesses of the Terror most strongly. He was staying in Zurich at the time for business reasons, and there he discussed the events and their interpretation with leading intellectuals, first and foremost with Fichte, who had just published a basically positive position statement on the French Revolution (Fichte, 1793). The issue was how a republic that had been basically approved of could be made stable without brutal authority of the state and despotism. At the end of 1792 Pestalozzi began writing a tract on the French Revolution that he finished in the fall of 1793 but never published, titled *Ja oder Nein* [Yes or No] (Pestalozzi, 1793/1931a). His commentary is revealing and somewhat surprising, as he says neither "yes" nor "no" and instead qualifies his answers. His position on the French Revolution is a "yes, but" and "no, not like that." The "yes" was owing to Pestalozzi's republican identity and thus his hope that France would become what Switzerland (in the eyes of Pestalozzi) had once been and should still be: a republic of virtue: "I compared the course of events to the ideals of my youth, dreamt, had great hopes, found myself deceived" (Pestalozzi, 1793/1931a, p. 105f.; freely translated here). The "no, not like that" refers to the fact that the modern republic, based on natural law rather than on virtue, was not seen as able to alter the problem of power and selfishness and thus the happiness of a republic.

The deception was self-deception, because Pestalozzi had compared the youthful ideals of the republic of virtue with a modern republic (fraught with difficulty) that was based on modern natural law and notions of social contract and had largely removed public virtue from the agenda of political importance. Recognizing his own false yardstick when judging the events led Pestalozzi (1793/1931a) to a solution of which only signs are visible in 1793 but which already clearly shows characteristics of German idealism. After sharply criticizing the distorted understanding of freedom by the French, which he saw as the result of centuries of oppression, Pestalozzi concluded that at present the exalted ideas of monarchical omnipotence—that is, the legitimation of absolute monarchy—had turned into exalted ideas of the right to political self-determination—that is, legitimation of tyranny of the people. However, Pestalozzi considered freedom to be far more than merely determining what should not be prohibited, and precisely at this point Pestalozzi emphasized the Protestant ideal of inwardness: political freedom was a good thing only if the individual had "a longing for inner refinement of the self"—that is, only if the individual was first of all a moral person (Pestalozzi, 1793/1931a, pp. 149–165). Freedom now no longer required only *Freiheitssinn*, or public virtue, as in Pestalozzi's ideals in the late 1770s; it now required inner moral decency (*Sittlichkeit*).

5.3 The political consequences in the mid-1790s

In contrast to Pestalozzi's political philosophy prior to the French Revolution, it was no longer only moral standards that were needed—along with laws and vocational education—for social integration of people but rather man's independent inwardness, the location of man's most core human freedom. This is a Protestant *topos* that played a central role mainly in German idealism, and it was probably conveyed to Pestalozzi by Fichte. This inner freedom reminded Pestalozzi of the early Christians, as he wrote in an unfinished work in 1794 (Pestalozzi, 1794/1931b), who seemed to him to be moral—not political—sans-culottes. The difference is subtle and decisive for social peace: "The first Christians seemed to have lived in moral sans-culotte-ism—that is, they gave voluntarily what bourgeois sans-culotte-ism steals; they let themselves be killed, whereas bourgeois sans-culotte-ism kills others" (Pestalozzi, 1794/1931b, p. 266; freely translated here). Therefore, the republic had to be based on the individual morality of people. This was an insight that Pestalozzi would soon apply to developments in Switzerland.

In Europe the events in France were met with ever greater skepticism by powerful people, but they stirred up hope among the disadvantaged. In particular, they added fuel to the reading societies that were founded around 1790 in the countryside of Zurich at the initiative of the rural upper classes. In Zurich, the "Reading Society at the Lake" founded by rich factory owners, surgeons, and various men in the town governments of the municipalities on the Lake of Zurich would become famous. This reading society was especially interested in the events in France, in particular in the *Strassburger Courier*, a publication that appeared twice a week and reported from Paris.

The members' reaction to the events in Paris was unique in Europe. Inspired by reading the revolutionary writings, the members of the Reading Society at the Lake began reading the history of their fatherland and searching for old sources showing that the countryside had originally had far more rights than was the case at the end of the eighteenth century. Through this, they gained insights into their original rights prior to the process of oligarchization of the city-state of Zurich, which had set in at the start of the eighteenth century. Their sources were the *Waldmannschen Spruchbriefe* (vowed constitutional letters originating from the mayor of Zurich, Hans Waldmann (1435–1489)) of 1489, in which the countryside and the city were stated to be practically equal, and the *Kappeler Briefe* written after Zwingli's death in 1531, which forbid the city to start any acts of war without the knowledge and wish of the countryside. The privileges set out in these documents had tacitly disappeared over the centuries.

These "documented" rights allowed the Zurich "subjects" to follow a different strategy in their demands for more rights than their fellow-sufferers in other European countries followed. Demands for more (economic) freedoms did not have to be limited to only natural law arguments and could instead cite historical facts. In the Stäfa region on the Lake of Zurich, an actual popular movement arose in 1794–1795 that invoked the old documented rights and caused a great deal of irritation in the city's elite. The city's response was extremely inept and unnecessarily brutal, resulting in the threat of a violent popular uprising. Encouraged by worried city residents, Pestalozzi traveled to the area of the unrest, where as a "man of the rural people" and at the same time a city citizen he was to mediate. He wrote a number of tracts in which he explicitly supported the demands for greater economic freedom of the rural population using historical and republic of virtue arguments, seeking to have a moderating effect on the city government but not succeeding, however. But he also had no success with the rural people, whom he told to exercise restraint, so as not to become enslaved to "exalted ideas of rights of the people," which he had blamed the French revolutionaries of doing. Specifically, he accused the spokesman of the underprivileged rural population of demanding additional economic freedom not to foster the common welfare but primarily to accumulate wealth for the few of them. As a disappointed Pestalozzi wrote in 1795, he had, namely, firmly believed that the leaders of the freedom movement had been acting not just as rich persons but rather "as members of your communities in your towns" and therefore had been "having in mind the common good and not personal advantage" (Pestalozzi, 1795/1931c, p. 306). The angry crowd saw Pestalozzi's warnings as a betrayal of their cause, and Pestalozzi was forced to flee the region in fear of his life.

5.4 Pestalozzi's *Meine Nachforschungen* (1797) on the eve of the Helvetic Revolution

The political philosophical discussions on the future of republics under the conditions of modern commerce and Pestalozzi's concrete experiences with the political unrest in Zurich motivated him to continue work on a treatise that he had started in 1793. In a letter to Philipp Emanuel von Fellenberg on 15 November 1793 he described this essay, quoting Fichte as "the philosophy of my politics" (Pestalozzi, 1793/1949, p. 303). The many drafts of the treatise that have been handed down are evidence of how Pestalozzi must have struggled with the fundamental principles of his political self-understanding before it was finally published in 1797 under the title *Meine Nachforschungen über die Entwicklung des Menschengeschlechts* [My Inquiries into the Course of Nature in the Development of Mankind] (Pestalozzi, 1797/1938). Even though the treatise received little attention for 100 years, it can be considered to be Pestalozzi's main philosophical work.

Meine Nachforschungen is divided into three sections. The first and last sections are noticeably similar: they deal with basic social political concepts such as freedom, justice, and property. The middle section contains a kind of anthropological analysis. The purpose of this noteworthy structure is to present in the first section the central social concepts from the perspective of egoistic persons, called *Parteimenschen* [biased, partisan persons] in order to suggest hopelessness of the political future, which Pestalozzi calls the "contradiction" of man. In the second section, however, he points out that these contradictory interpretations that lead men into political hopelessness are not inherent in society per se but instead lie in the nature of man. The nature of man is not a uniform thing but rather is dual or threefold. As natural and social beings, people can do nothing other than to interpret the fundamental social concepts as working to their own personal advantage. And because everyone does that, no political consensus can be reached that benefits all. The point is, however, that man has also a third nature that differs fundamentally from his first two natures (natural and social). It is his moral nature: "I possess a power in myself to imagine all things of this world for myself, independently of my animal desire/eagerness and of my social circumstances" (Pestalozzi, 1797/1938, p. 105; freely translated here). If people view freedom, justice, property, and so on from this third perspective, they see them completely differently, selflessly, and in the service of the truth—that is, with a view to the common good. The third section of *Meine Nachforschungen* is based on these insights. It goes through each of the basic social concepts mentioned in the first section and asks how they must appear to natural man, social man, and moral man. Pestalozzi leaves no doubt that only the moral world view, the selfless attitude to the world—moral sans-culotte-ism—guarantees politics that do not work for privileges of the rich and powerful few but rather for the welfare of all. The contradictions in which man finds himself hopelessly entangled in the first section of *Meine Nachforschungen* thus turn out to be an illusionary construction of persons who are not moral and thus cause so much suffering and injustice.

Recognizing the threefold structure of human nature will bring people in harmony with themselves and make it possible for them to have a selfless world view. Pestalozzi presents the threefold nature of man not only as layered vertically but also as "shifted" horizontally. Here he uses the analogy of human development and individual development—that is, phylogenesis and ontogenesis. According to this construction, in childhood the small child is as determined by his natural nature and the will to survive as the pre-social wild child is, which results in the problematic "egoism." In agreement with Pestalozzi's position in the 1780s, the epoch of the social contract is not seen as an expression of humanity or philanthropy but rather primarily as a means to more simply and securely satisfy man's needs through property. What is decisive is that the social state—adolescence—does not change man's natural selfishness. This means that the laws that are essential for protection of property always seem to people to be disliked constraints that they are in favor of for others but not so much for themselves. Only the higher phase of development, the *Meisteralter* [age of a master (in the sense of a master craftsman)], when persons can overcome their egoistic view of things, brings with it an essentially benevolent and not egoistic attitude towards social life (Pestalozzi, 1797/1938, p. 107).

In the horizontal shifting of the vertically layered three natures of man there is an educational concept, although in *Meine Nachforschungen* it is little developed. The objective is that the first education, that of the natural nature, is natural movement and physical strengthening; the second education, that of social life, is characterized by vocational education that entails strong socialization and restricts egoism. The seed of the third education, which starts with family love and ends with the morality of the individual person, can only sprout once the social education, the vocational socialization, has accomplished the "maiming" of the selfish nature of man (Pestalozzi, 1797/1938, p. 93). Thus, the republic of virtue is now based on people whose moral worldview has been made possible by strict vocational education that curbs man's egoistic nature and by the later fruits of familial love.

Notes

1 Wilhelm von Humboldt (1767–1835) played an important role in the Prussian government after 1806, after the defeat of Prussia Army by the forces of Napoleon I of France. In particular, Humboldt was one of the founders of the university in Berlin, Germany, which carries his and his brother's (Alexander) name today (Humboldt-Universität zu Berlin) and became a model for modern research universities (also in the United States). Humboldt also worked on the theory of *Bildung*, a theory of education that was based on the ideal of a purposeless, aesthetically educated soul and that was to be strictly distinct from purposeful education for usefulness; see http://en.wikipedia.org/wiki/Wilhelm_von_Humboldt

2 Joachim Heinrich Campe (1746–1818), held in high regard in Germany, was one of the Enlightenment pedagogues, who sought to convey Lutheran

Protestant morality and usefulness and propagated corresponding school reforms; see http://en.wikipedia.org/wiki/Joachim_Heinrich_Campe

3 The French revolutionists were convinced that their new freedom was not limited to France but applied to the world, and by nominating further freedom fighters around the world they were trying to define an idealistic network of men devoted to human freedom. It seems that Pestalozzi was honored for his commitment to the rural people in his novel *Lienhard und Getrud* (1781).

6
The Helvetic Republic and the Discovery of "the Method"

Abstract: *In 1798 Switzerland was overrun by the French revolutionary armies and became subject to the logic of the French Revolution. The proclaiming of the Helvetic Republic in 1798 fanned the hopes of many critics of the conditions of the Old Swiss Confederation that the ideals that they thought to have found in the early history of the free communes—the republic of virtues and brotherhood— could be reestablished. In the firm conviction that the new republic supported by France would be headed by wiser power holders, Pestalozzi submitted a request to the Helvetic unity government only a few weeks after the revolution. He was sent to Stans in central Switzerland to educate children of war victims. This experience laid the foundation for his later successes, for it was here that for the first time that Pestalozzi's "method" became visible. When the institution in Stans had to be closed a half-year later, supporters of Pestalozzi made efforts to have him installed as a school teacher in the progressive town of Burgdorf, so that he could further develop his "method."*

Tröhler, Daniel. *Pestalozzi and the Educationalization of the World*. New York: Palgrave Macmillan, 2013.
DOI: 10.1057/9781137346858.

The events of the French Revolution did not remain restricted to France. The Declaration of the Rights of Man and Citizen on August 26, 1789 reinforced on the European continent, and brought into position again absolutist monarchies, the principles that had already been set out in the Declaration of Independence of the American colonists and that now gained currency in Europe also: the absolutists states saw themselves in existential danger, not least due to the fact that in 1794 some of those in power in France attempted to quiet turbulence at home by declaring war against other countries. In the name of exporting the revolution, French troops attacked the Austrian Netherlands, which were under control of the House of Habsburg. As a result, the Batavian Republic was proclaimed in 1795,[1] followed one year later in northern Italy by the founding of the Cispadane Republic (in 1796).[2] The republic as a form of government was now on everyone's lips, in part desired but mostly feared. Europe faced fundamental change, change that most of those in power fought against by all available means. Since the rapid successes of the French troops did not have the desired effect at home, and the domestic turmoil continued,[3] the strategy of declaring war against other states was thought at first to be just a flash in the pan, until Napoleon Bonaparte staged a coup d'état and seized power in France, after having had great successes on Europe's battlefields. Napoleon would fundamentally change Europe and (indirectly) create the political bases upon which in 1830 the educationalization of social problems, which had been conceived by intellectuals, officials, and wealthy citizens towards 1800, became institutionalized with fundamental reforms of the schools in the individual nation states that would eventually become founded after the defeat of Napoleon, respectively the Congress of Vienna (1814–1815).

In 1798 Switzerland was overrun by the French revolutionary armies and became subject to the logic of the French Revolution and had to adopt the political order of the French Republic. Immediately after the proclaiming of the Helvetic Republic Pestalozzi submitted a request to the Helvetic unity government, offering his expertise in the education of the poor, and asking for financial help for a reopening of the Neuhof institute. He was sent to Stans in central Switzerland to educate children of war victims. This experience in Stans laid the foundation for his later successes, for it was here that for the first time Pestalozzi's "method" became visible, an idea of education and instruction, that would make him, only a few years later, famous all over Europe.

6.1 The Helvetic Republic in 1798 and hopes for reestablishment of the old republic of virtue

The eighteenth century brought a certain degree of oligarchization not only in Zurich but also in many parts of the Old Swiss Confederation, so that towards the end of the century not only the rural population of Zurich but also large parts of the "subject territories" as well as the committed reform circles had become dissatisfied with the state of the land. The French Revolution with its natural law argumentation, according to which every person has basic rights that cannot be revoked, must have been met with great interest. Even though there were great differences between the two types of republics—in France the republic was based on natural rights and the idea of the social contract, whereas the Swiss understanding proceeded from the assumption that virtue was the core and that there should be rule by the best and most worthy (meritocracy)—the relevant arguments from its neighboring country to the west had a serious impact on Switzerland. In the winter of 1797–1798 unrest increased in various parts of Switzerland, and the invasion of the French troops and two small skirmishes against poorly organized and not exactly heroic militiamen near Bern marked the end of the Old Confederation.[4] Although many arguments that spoke for fundamental changes were guided by the French model, the ideal of the old republic of virtue continued to exist—that is, the way that people saw the old freedom struggles of the fourteenth century, which they reckoned to have been virtuous and fraternal. On the legal side, there was the model of the rational, natural law based French Republic, but in the minds of the Swiss, the old idea of the republic of virtue lived on. This would lead to numerous conflicts.

However, militarily and formally, the Revolution as a military and political event that occurred far more quickly than the mental dispositions or fundamental attitudes of a large part of the population could have changed. In addition to the old holders of power as well as the reformers, who like Pestalozzi adhered to the old republic of virtue, it was mainly the Catholic conservative parts of the Old Confederation that refused to accept the new government. This was not only because a centuries-long tradition of strong federalism with correspondingly high regional autonomy was going to be replaced by a unity government but also because the new state, following the French model, was going to be secular—that is, church and state would become separate. At this point in time, in the spring of 1798, the new Helvetic government asked Pestalozzi the writer to make the new constitution appealing to the Swiss people. Receiving an official commission for the first time in his life, Pestalozzi went to work immediately and delivered a short pamphlet, titled *Zuruf an die vormals demokratischen Kantone* [Call to the Formerly Democratic Cantons] (Pestalozzi, 1798/1938) within days.[5] In the pamphlet, Pestalozzi constantly addresses the Swiss as either "friends and brothers" or "sons of the Tells[6] and Winkelrieds,"[7] whom he beseeched to accept the new constitution, so that "we can once again raise ourselves to the spirit of the first founders of our confederation, which seeks only to be free and to free true brothers" (Pestalozzi, 1798/1938, p. 281; freely translated here). The new constitution, which was strongly modeled on the French constitution, was to make it possible for the old republic of virtue to be reestablished.

Pestalozzi's role as a national writer was only a temporary occupation. Before being appointed as national peacemaker writer, Pestalozzi had already contacted the new government asking to be supported in his educational aims. He cleverly connected the new government to his educational purposes by defining the need of the new republic for better education: "Convinced, that the fatherland urgently needs a considerable improvement in education and schools for the lowest classes of the people, and most certain that three- to four monthly experiments would discover and prove the most important results" with regards to these aims, Pestalozzi offered his services to the new Helvetic directorate (Pestalozzi 1798/1951, p. 15; freely translated here). By "the lowest classes of the people," Pestalozzi did not mean persons in squalid poverty but rather the large class of persons who owned no land, whose children would become farmhands and servants, and who thus did not conform to the ideal of by-and-large economic independence. These addressees were thus more similar to those that he had served at Neuhof in the 1770s or, a bit more inclusive in terms of social distinction, in *Lienhard und Gertrud*. Pestalozzi had in mind education that aimed primarily at occupations and that would secure people a livelihood, without which no socially relevant virtue could be reached. The opportunity for realization was to come soon, even if under extremely difficult conditions.

In the meantime, all the efforts of the new central government to convince the cantons in central Switzerland to cooperate failed. When all persuasion efforts had to be deemed futile, French troops stationed in the country invaded the bastion of the resistance, Nidwalden[8] with its capital town Stans, and rapidly caused massive devastation with many casualties. The troops left behind them an intimidated population as well as poverty, orphans, and half-orphans, and the new government had to act if it were to be seen as legitimate. At that moment, the government "remembered" Pestalozzi's educational aspirations and sent him to Stans to take charge of the children. Pestalozzi, now 52 years old, was very happy to accept this commission, inspite of skepticism on the part of many, including his own family.

Pestalozzi's wife Anna commented in her diary: "In 1798 Pestalozzi was called to Stans as supervisor of the many children who in the sad battle had lost their parents because they had not wanted to accept the new constitution" (as quoted in Schulthess, 1993, p. 35f.). Although she had warned Pestalozzi not to take on too much at his age, he traveled to Stans. A letter that he wrote to her from Stans shows how much Pestalozzi must have suffered under the long years of isolation previously:

> The question as to what my and your fate will be cannot be doubtful for much longer. I am undertaking one of the greatest ideas of the time. If you have a husband who is deserving of the contempt and disparagement with which he has been generally treated, then there will be no deliverance for us. But if I have been misjudged, and if I am worthy of what I myself believe in, you can soon expect help and advice from me. But for now be still—every word from you burdens my heart. (as quoted in Schulthess, 1993, p. 35f.)

6.2 The experiment in Stans

It cannot be said that Pestalozzi, as a Reformed Protestant, supporter of the new government, and honorary French citizen, was really welcome in the invasion-ravaged Stans, despite his humanitarian commission to take care of the children of the war victims using funds from the central government. The fact that the orphanage was set up in a wing of the convent (a monastery exclusively for women) at Stans also did not increase acceptance. Acceptance was so low that officers had to catch some of the children and bring them to Pestalozzi by force, often with the result that they—well-fed and freshly clothed—disappeared again. Having very little experience and no teaching assistants to help him, Pestalozzi's start as head of a home for children was not encouraging, particularly as infrastructure conditions were most inadequate, making a focus on vocational education impossible. Still, Stans would become—at least in the historiography (and hagiography!) of education—the dramatic turning point in history, the crucial point between modern education philosophy, which began with Rousseau, and the modern school that became widely established after 1800 (Soëtard, 1981).

It says something about Pestalozzi's impressive energy and desperation that he not only held out but also was able to lay the foundation for his further career in the short seven months that the children's home at Stans was in existence (from December 1798 to June 1799). Not least owing to the support of the nuns at the convent and of the monks at the monastery at the other end of the town, Pestalozzi gradually succeeded in gaining the trust of the children and then the toleration of the parents. He was a teacher, master, and father all rolled into one; he rejected both outside help and the scientific knowledge of the time. In his belief that what the children primarily needed was love, he saw "academically" guided teaching and methodology as far-flown and unrealistic. Instead, everything was to develop out of a harmonious family idyll. Whatever could arise out of the "natural condition" had to be "good" and as such help to improve the "rotten" world. The children "were out of the world, they were out of Stans; they were with me, and I was with them," Pestalozzi later wrote in his famous "Stans letter" (Pestalozzi, 1807/1932, p. 9).

Accordingly, the children's education, at least according to the Stans letter written in 1807 by a now famous Pestalozzi (there are unfortunately no other sources for Pestalozzi's time in Stans), had three parts, which can be seen to correspond only partly with the three natures of man in Pestalozzi's *Meine Nachforschungen*. The basis of his approach is love, which in the child is developed through satisfying the child's primary needs for emotional and physical warmth, nourishment, and clothing and which produces a certain state of inner composure (*Gemütsstimmung*)—in other words the soul. "I was convinced that my heart would change the general condition of my children in the same way that the sun in springtime changes the condition of the frozen winter soil" (Pestalozzi, 1807/1932, p. 6, freely translated here). This composure is then the basis upon which the children—even if not always out of pure joy, which is why they need guidance, warning, and practice at "overcoming" (p. 17)—develop a way and practice of life through which they themselves come upon "great truths" (p. 23). Very much in the style of an anti-Enlightenment philosophy and education,[9] Pestalozzi rails against the formal transmission of rational and moral contents, because they would always remain only "superficial" (p. 26). For this reason, intellectual education requires this inner composure as well as a moral practice of life and is merely the attempt to verbalize the great truths that are discovered intuitively out of a morally refined way of life: "Vitalized emotions of virtue had to precede the verbal reflection about these virtues" (p. 16). Language teaching is thus the teaching of the formulation of pre-linguistically perceived truths, truths that evolved from love and love's consequences. Vocational education, which Pestalozzi had originally wanted to pursue, was not completely absent in the Stans experiment, but in his reflections it was dealt with theoretically only marginally. The focus in Stans was elementary moral education, as Pestalozzi (1807/1932) wrote further in the Stans letter, expressing the educational turn of his time, finding certainty in the educationalized soul:

> Elementary moral education, considered as a whole, includes three aspects: the children's moral inner composure and moral sense must first be aroused by pure feelings; then the children must be exercised in moral practice through self-control and effort to engage in the just and good; finally, they must be brought to form, by reflection and comparison, a moral outlook, a notion of the rights and moral conditions in which they live by virtue of their environment. (p. 19)

Contemporary reports described Pestalozzi as an extremely committed head of the children's home but as a man who in his total devotion exhausted himself and was not open to any suggestions or help. There were subsequently tensions with the authorities, and when in the early summer of 1799 a part of the war on the European continent took place in Switzerland, the Helvetic government in central Switzerland, for lack of an alternative, turned Pestalozzi's building over to the French troops, who needed a place for their wounded. This decision caused Pestalozzi to have a breakdown, and he left Stans to recover for several weeks at an Alpine health resort (Gurnigel) near Bern. But this did not end his educational ambitions, and fate would have it that the Helvetic Republic urgently needed mass schooling and a new school method, which it believed to have found with Pestalozzi.

6.3   Burgdorf: "the method"

The term "the method," or "the Pestalozzi method," which for a long time stood for all of Pestalozzi's education and at the same time functioned as a magic word in its time, playing a significant role in making Pestalozzi famous throughout Europe, was not coined by Pestalozzi himself but by Philipp Albert Stapfer (1766–1840),[10] who had studied Protestant theology and was the Helvetic minister of education and a supporter of Pestalozzi. Stapfer had the thankless job of setting up a new school system in the middle of the turmoil of war and with empty state coffers. Not only were there no trained personnel available for a new school system but also no modern educational method. As the question arose as to what was to happen with Pestalozzi after the unhappy end of Stans in June 1799, Stapfer decided to go with Pestalozzi when it came to the Helvetic school issue. However, Pestalozzi had made himself very unpopular with the Helvetic government in 1798 when he wrote on the subject of fair taxation and put forward some radical suggestions that irritated wealthy citizens and influential people. Stapfer defended his championing of Pestalozzi in 1799 to the national executive by stating that Pestalozzi had found "a method" that would allow students to learn to read very easily: "He has discovered a very simple method by which children can learn to read"; he has resolved the special difficulties in this teaching area by basing his method precisely "on the nature of the child's mind" (as quoted Luginbühl, 1902, p. 187f.; freely translated here). The focus was no longer on vocational education of underprivileged people in the bosom of an ethically legitimized state, towards which Pestalozzi wanted to contribute, but rather on a method of teaching reading that was based on the child's mind and the child's development—that is, based on psychological laws.

But before Pestalozzi would become head of an educational institute at Burgdorf Castle, several obstacles had to be overcome. In the 13 months between the closing of Stans and the move into the Burgdorf Castle in July 1800, Pestalozzi had a teaching position in the town of Burgdorf, with varying success. As it so happened, the designated Helvetic head of teacher training, Johann Rudolf Fischer (1772–1800) had chosen Burgdorf Castle for a Helvetic teacher training college, but he died in May 1800 before the college could be opened. Moreover, a number of war refugee children from eastern Switzerland had been brought to Burgdorf in the safer canton of Bern under the direction of a young teacher, Hermann Krüsi (1775–1844),[11] in the spring of 1800.[12] When Pestalozzi petitioned the Helvetic government in June 1800 to let him have the castle as a private institute, where he would teach, bring up poor children, and train teachers, the building was turned over to him. It was here at Burgdorf Castle that Pestalozzi gained educational fame.

At the very beginning of their years at Burgdorf, however, Pestalozzi and his wife Anna had to cope with the death of their only child, Hans Jakob, in 1801. Anna Pestalozzi-Schulthess described the death of their son in her diary and mentioned also Pestalozzi's new job:

> Our dear only child died in the evening of 15 August at eight o'clock. In the month of May he had such a serious bout of his illness that I...was called home [to Neuhof].... Finally, he became weaker and weaker, and his attacks became different than previously. His tongue was now affected, and his memory was so weak that the whole time he could only speak some words.... A great task that his dear father had taken on, educating young people in Burgdorf, prevented this dear, good husband from seeing him again. (Schulthess, 1993, p. 45f.; freely translated here)

Helping Pestalozzi in the realization of this "great task" was a society founded by Stapfer in June 1800, the *Gesellschaft von Freunden des Erziehungswesens* [society of the friends of education]. The society urged Pestalozzi to present the foundations of "his method" to the public. The result was Pestalozzi's book, *Wie Gertrud ihre Kinder lehrt* (How Gertrude Teaches Her Children) (Pestalozzi, 1801/1932),[13] which takes the form of 14 "letters." The argumentation in the first four letters is autobiographical. Pestalozzi writes of his difficult, sorely afflicted life in order to illustrate that the unique combination of originally inherited naivety and tough life experiences led him to discover the "natural course" in education. This natural course is presented systematically in the next 10 letters, with letters 5 through 10 focusing on the natural education of man's cognitive faculties. Pestalozzi derives the principle of naturalness from the circumstance that people are always in concrete surroundings and can learn from and through them—a circumstance that he describes educationally as the principle of "sense-impression," or observation (*Anschauung*). Sense-impression is the fundamental of all instruction/knowledge, which itself is divided into three elements: the form, the number, and the notion of things. This reduction of instruction to the three elements corresponds to the child's own capacities, which themselves are pre-shaped by a natural developmental course that is triggered by (ordered) encountering of the outside world. The principle of sense-impression, or observation, thus functions as a bridge between the external world and the child's inner developmental principle. But the outer world must not appear chaotic; to this purpose, the world must be brought before the eyes of the child in a well-ordered way. This is a concept that Pestalozzi would expand upon in the following years in his textbooks.

But there was more. Cognitive development was not to take place on its own but rather as embedded in the development of other human faculties—namely, physical education, which Pestalozzi (1801/1932) discusses in the twelfth letter of *Wie Gertrud ihre Kinder lehrt*, and especially moral-religious education, which is the subject of letters 13 and 14. Here the mother–child relationship is extolled as the foundation of all religious education and thus of all true human education: "The core from which the feelings rise that are the essence of worship of God and morality... emanates completely from the natural relationship between the under-age child and his mother" (p. 350). It is mothers who see to it that the real world, which is "not God's first creation" (meaning that the real world is rotten), does not come before the child's eyes as "a world full of lies and deception" (p. 350). In this way, mothers are preservers of the good in people, and they are responsible for their development of morality and religiousness. Against the background of a completely corrupt world, the good in the world—the republic of virtue—lies in the hands of (loving) mothers: in Pestalozzi's conception, the educationalization of social problems is basically a motherly affair. The resulting harmony of the three human powers and faculties, the powers of the head, the heart, and the hand, which is possible only through the pre-eminence of the powers of the heart, is for Pestalozzi the aim of "the method" that he promised to the world after 1800. And the world was ready to listen to this message and to see Pestalozzi as its savior, which is also how he liked to see himself.

Notes

1. http://en.wikipedia.org/wiki/Batavian_Republic
2. http://en.wikipedia.org/wiki/Cispadane_Republic
3. For example, the War in the Vendée; see http://en.wikipedia.org/wiki/War_in_the_Vendée
4. See http://en.wikipedia.org/wiki/Battle_of_Grauholz
5. In contrast to the large cantons like Bern or Zurich, which were a mixture of aristocracy and democracy (democracy limited to the citizens of the capital), the very rural cantons of central Switzerland had extended democratic rights to all citizens of the territory. The sovereign took its decision at the *Landsgemeinde* see http://en.wikipedia.org/wiki/Landsgemeinde

6   Referring to Wilhelm Tell, the great Swiss hero of freedom. See http://en.wikipedia.org/wiki/William_Tell
7   Referring to Arnold Winkelried, another mythical hero of freedom. See http://en.wikipedia.org/wiki/Arnold_von_Winkelried
8   The principles of the French Revolution were rather unpopular in some parts of the Swiss cantons, including Nidwalden. Like other cantons in central Switzerland, Nidwalden was accustomed to self-government. When rebel forces threatened the new Helvetic Republic by refusing to accept the new centralized constitution, Nidwalden was attacked by French troops on September 9, 1798. The canton's infrastructure was damaged, and at least 400 people were killed.
9   After 1790—after the French Revolution—a strong anti-Enlightenment movement arose in Germany that led eventually into either German idealism or the German Romantic movement. Georg Heinrich Ludwig Nicolovius (1767–1839) belonged to this movement led by Johann Georg Hamann (1730–1788) (https://en.wikipedia.org/wiki/Johann_Georg_Hamann) and by Friedrich Heinrich Jacobi (1743–1819) (http://en.wikipedia.org/wiki/Friedrich_Heinrich_Jacobi). Nicolovius became acquainted with Pestalozzi on his tour through Europe in 1791. He and Jacobi exchanged letters with Pestalozzi discussing questions of materialism and (Christian) idealism; they suspected Pestalozzi of being exposed to the former in his novels *Lienhard and Gertrud*. This exchange of letters is symptomatic of the difference in social philosophy between Lutheranism and Zwinglianism, the latter including social (and thus material) aspects of life in the design of the good life (Nicolovius, 1792/2009; Nicolovius, 1794/2009; Jacobi, 1794/2009; Pestalozzi, 1793/1949; Pestalozzi, 1794/1998).
10 http://en.wikipedia.org/wiki/Philipp_Albert_Stapfer
11 His son, Hermann Krüsi, Jr. (1817–1903), became important in the dissemination of the Pestalozzi method first in London, from 1853 in Boston, and then from 1862 as director of the Oswego Primary Teachers' Training School (today: State University of New York at Oswego); see http://en.wikipedia.org/wiki/Oswego_Movement
12 The War of the Second Coalition (1798–1802) between France and the European monarchs was fought to a large part in Switzerland and resulted in massive destruction and many war refugees. See http://en.wikipedia.org/wiki/War_of_the_Second_Coalition
13 The first English translation, *How Gertrude Teaches Her Children: An Attempt to Help Mothers to Teach their Own Children and an Account of the Method*, was published in 1894 in London (by Swan Sonnenschein) and Syracuse, New York (by C. W. Bardeen), edited by Ebenezer Cooke and translated by Lucy E. Holland and Frances C. Turner. Several new editions followed.

7
Propaganda and Institutional Success

Abstract: *In the emerging educationalized culture of the time, the new republics felt the need of a new educational system with new educational methods. The authorities of the Helvetic Republic believed that Pestalozzi's way of teaching—developed in Stans—was a true innovation because it was guided by the natural development of the human mind, it was quick and easy, and it needed no preconditions. Furthermore, it was believed to strengthen the self-esteem of the student making this way of teaching appropriate for the entire curriculum of the education system that was yet to be developed. An impressive state propaganda relaunched Pestalozzi's career (Pestalozzi was now 55 years old) and led him to liken his so far unsuccessful life to the suffering of Jesus Christ.*

Tröhler, Daniel. *Pestalozzi and the Educationalization of the World*. New York: Palgrave Macmillan, 2013.
DOI: 10.1057/9781137346858.

7.1 State propaganda for and institutional successes of "the Pestalozzi method"

The Society of the Friends of Education founded in June 1800 by Stapfer, the Helvetic minister of education, not only urged Pestalozzi to publish the foundations of "his method" in *How Gertrude Teaches Her Children* (Pestalozzi, 1801/1932) but also sought to have the method evaluated by an independent party. They secured the services of Johann Samuel Ith (1747–1813), a respected and philosophically trained dean, who—after turning down a position as home secretary of the Helvetic Republic—was appointed president of the state school board of Bern. Ith visited Pestalozzi in Burgdorf and wrote a report that was to be printed and distributed. In the report, Ith (1802) stressed six points that were all intended to put "the Pestalozzi method" in the best light: first, Pestalozzi's way of teaching was new and consequently a true discovery, having no precursors. Second, the method was guided by the natural development of the human mind, so that it was based on developmental psychology. Third, due to this basis, teaching became quick and easy, and fourth, the method thus required of both teacher and student no knowledge or skills but only healthy senses. Fifth, the sure success of this method reinforced students' self-esteem and through this fostered also their self-satisfaction, which in turn promoted morality. And sixth, this way of teaching was not limited to merely elementary school subjects but, rather, was for all school subjects including religion. Ith (1802) concluded:

> With this new teaching method, the true elementary instruction has been found... that gives the child preliminary exercise in everything, prepares the child for all arts and sciences, can be used with all social groups and classes, and as the first foundation is indispensable for complete *Menschenbildung*. [shaping of the whole human character] (p. VIII; freely translated here)

At the request of Ith, who prepared the report, the national executive of the Helvetic Republic resolved in 1802 to give Pestalozzi an advance of 8,000 francs for the printing of (planned) elementary books on teaching, to copyright the books, to commission Pestalozzi to set up a national teachers college, to grant Pestalozzi and his staff a guaranteed wage, and—and this was the most important for Pestalozzi's success as an author—to publish Ith's report and to send it with a recommendation and in quadruplicate to all school boards and school inspectors in Switzerland, together with 25 copies of subscription announcements for Pestalozzi's—not yet written—"elementary books." On this basis, propaganda developed that targeted a group that was remarkably receptive to the promise of "the method" and whose response was accordingly euphoric.

Pestalozzi's success was not undisputed, but the competitors in this emerging educationalized world, such as Johann Rudolf Steinmüller (1773–1835) of St Gallen, dealt with Pestalozzi so roughly that they angered their own few sympathizers (Steinmüller, 1803). The very fact that there was competition shows that after the fall of the Ancien Régime, a more or less free education market had formed in which the suppliers tried to convince those in power of the quality of their product and courted the favor of political protection through personal relationships and journalistic tricks. With the help of the propaganda, quite a lot of private schools were established under the Pestalozzi label starting already in 1802 in Switzerland. Some of them had nothing to do with "the Pestalozzi method," which they could not have had anyway, so long as, first, the method still referred primarily to mothers and, second, parents paying school tuition demanded clear results. The results that parents were mostly looking for were not the "shaping of the whole human character" but instead successful transmission of skills and knowledge. These successful private schools became a problem for the public schools of the Helvetic Republic. In Stäfa in the Canton of Zurich, for instance, parents passed an impromptu decision at an improvised town meeting in 1803, without informing the state school board, to suspend the present teacher and to appoint in his place as the official teacher the extremely popular private teacher, who allegedly or in fact taught according to "the Pestalozzi method." This resulted in a reprimand by the state school board, but the cantonal authorities also resolved to send future prospective teachers to Pestalozzi for training in the method.

Ith's evaluation report published in 1802 immediately had a large circulation. Shortly thereafter it was reported everywhere that the Helvetic government had given Pestalozzi an advance and a copyright for books. The first book on the method appeared that same year— namely, Johann Friedrich Herbart's[1] (1802) *Pestalozzi's Idee eines ABC der Anschauung* [Pestalozzi's Idea of the ABCs of Sense-Impression]. Overall, the book had little to do with Pestalozzi and a lot to do with Herbart's attempt, by referring to the principle of sense-impression, to make mathematics the foundation of all instruction. One year later, Pestalozzi was already so popular that the periodical *Journal des Luxus und der*

Moden [Journal for Luxury and Fashion] published in Weimar, Germany, described the elementary books, which had not yet gone into print, as the latest trend in Europe ("Neueste Mode," 1803)! Also in 1803, in addition to three instruction methods books by Pestalozzi (Pestalozzi 1803a, 1803b, 1803–1804), two other monographs on Pestalozzi were published in German (Soyaux, 1803; Himly, 1803) and one in Danish (Plum, 1803). These publications heated up the media coverage even more, so that after 1804 there was an explosion of works on Pestalozzi that can hardly be summarized and that were mainly rather dramatic and impassioned.

7.2 Period of suffering and redemption

With a few exceptions, all of these works on Pestalozzi—approving and rejecting—had similar characteristics. First, they almost always mentioned Ith's report, which had given "the new method" a promising start with its official propaganda. They then reproduced Pestalozzi's own description of his life (an essential part in Pestalozzi, 1801/1932; see below), which he interpreted as a story of suffering in his own commitment to social work: "Since the years of his youth," Pestalozzi's heart had "yearned to damn up the source of misery in which I saw the people around me sunken," and already 30 years previously he had "taken the work in hand" with which he was now engaged in as an educationalist (Pestalozzi, 1801/1932, p. 183). He had "lived together with more than 50 beggar children at Neuhof" and "shared his bread with them in poverty." He had turned himself into a beggar to teach the poor children to live as human beings even in the beggar state, guiding their education towards farming, proto-industry, and trade. Still today he saw no error in the fundaments of that approach; only the details had not yet been properly worked out, so that his plan had had to finally fail (p. 183f.). However, that failure had been salutary, insofar as his great financial difficulties at Neuhof had led himself into "misery," giving him "the in-depth knowledge of the misery of the people and its sources that no happy man knows" (p. 184):

> I suffered as the people suffered, and the people showed me what it was like and how no others saw it. For many long years, I sat among the people like an owl among birds. But in the midst of the scornful laughter of those who were dismissive of me, in the midst of their loud cry—You miserable wretch! You are less able to help yourself than the worst day laborer, and you imagine

that you can help the people?—in the midst of this scornful jeering, which I read on everyone's lips, the powerful river of my heart never stopped striving towards my sole goal of plugging the source of this misery in which I saw the people around me sunken, and from one side my strength increased more and more. My misfortune taught me more and more truth for my purpose. That which deceived no one always deceived me, but that which deceived everyone no longer deceived me. (Pestalozzi, 1801/1932, p. 184)

The allegory of the owl and the birds was not by chance; it underlined the role of the wise man who is not understood. The owl is not only a metaphor for wisdom; in ornithology, if owls come out in the daytime, they are attacked by crows and other birds. This meant that not only the high society had distanced itself from Pestalozzi but also his target group, the poor. The result was, in the logic of Pestalozzi's narrative, his total social isolation.

In Pestalozzi's account, it was only with the Helvetic Republic (proclaimed in 1798, ending in 1803), when he offered his services as a teacher, that others had bestowed him with their trust. They had sent him to Stans, where—as a "result of necessity"—the method became tangible and concrete, as Stapfer had witnessed and reported to the national executive. But the world still viewed him very skeptically, as Pestalozzi (1801/1932) wrote, and to demonstrate this skepticism he published a transcript of a conversation about him in the first letter of *How Gertrude Teaches Her Children*:

> The first said: "Do you see how ugly he is?"
>
> The other: "Yes, I am sorry for the poor fool."
>
> The first: "And so am I; but he cannot be helped. If ever he throws out a spark one moment, so that one might think he really is capable of something, the next moment it is again dark around him; and when one comes near him, he has only burnt himself."
>
> The other: "What a pity he did not burn himself to death! He cannot be helped till he is ashes."
>
> The first: "God knows, we must soon wish that for him."
>
> That was the reward of my work in Stanz; a work that perhaps no mortal ever attempted on such a scale and under such circumstances, and of which the inner result brought me practically to the point at which I now stand. (p. 192)

The affinity with Jesus Christ's life of suffering and the promise of redemption led almost automatically to the use of Biblical language when "the method" and its discoverer were discussed. Even Pestalozzi set out to determine whether the Gospel of Matthew was in agreement with his "method," and he made the following interpretation (1802/1952):

Now when His disciples had come to the other side, they had forgotten to take bread. Then Jesus said to them, "Take heed and beware of the leaven of the Pharisees and the Sadducees." Matthew 16:5–6	He [Jesus] warns his disciples against the styles of teaching, of even the most enlightened, most civilized, and most renowned men of his time formally appointed to the highest Church positions, and explains that their style of teaching was based on the decay of human nature rather than on the inward divine essence.(Pestalozzi, 1802/1952, p. 36)

7.3   Success abroad and the Pestalozzi cult

Interestingly, the biographical elaboration of the discovery of "the method," which Pestalozzi had himself utilized in *How Gertrude Teaches Her Children*, took off even with skeptical visitors to Burgdorf, who criticized "the method" as a method of schooling and instruction but still praised the "spirit" of the method, such as Adolf Soyaux (Soyaux, 1803), a Prussian theologian. The first secondary literature in 1802 and 1803, Ith's report published in 1802, and Pestalozzi's *Wie Gertrud ihre Kinder lehrt* (Pestalozzi, 1801/1932) were subsequently described and commentated on in dozens of articles and hundreds of pages in the popular press, and the commentaries themselves became the subject of critiques. Between 1801, the point in time when Pestalozzi first presented his method publicly in *Wie Gertrud ihre Kinder lehrt*, and 1805, a total of approximately 200 titles were published on Pestalozzi, ranging from simple announcements to comprehensive books. The first dissertation on Pestalozzi (Ziemssen, 1804), written by a theologian named Theodor Ziemssen, was published as early as in 1804. Most of the popular media were firmly in the hands of the Pestalozzians. This was true not only of *Der Neue Teutsche Merkur*—edited by Christoph Martin Wieland (1733–1813) in Weimar—in which as early as at the end of 1801 an anonymous letter on a visit to Burgdorf appeared. In the letter, "the method" was praised as the epitome of general refinement of human beings without "charlatanism" and "metaphysics," applicable everywhere and in all times, that shaped not primarily scholars but true human beings and for this reason transcended all social classes

("Auszug," 1801, p. 159). The same picture holds true of the journal *Neue Berlinische Monatsschrift*. In an essay in that journal (Riemann, 1804), Karl Friedrich Riemann, pastor and teacher of the poor, accused Pestalozzi of seeking to dissolve all social bonds and to circumvent religious education through his educational method. Johann Erich Biester, the editor of the journal, published the essay but along with a preliminary note and a long commentary that mentioned the many positive reports and responded to the danger of an amoral education through Pestalozzi's method as follows: "The fact that a good thinker that lacks morality is dangerous—of that is no one more fervently convinced than the author of *Lienhard und Gertrud*" (Biester, 1804, p. 143).

The strategy in *How Gertrude Teaches Her Children* of propagating the dignity of the method via Pestalozzi's biography and, with its title, of cashing in on the great literary success of *Lienhard und Gertrud*, proved successful. The worried Europeans wanted common public education, but education that would not call into question what appeared to be the last sure thing that one had—namely, religious certainty. The new had to combine with the old, and a new leader whose life apparently had so many similarities with the founder of Christendom could not be wrong, at least not in the basics. The educationalist and writer Johann Ludwig Ewald (1747–1822) wrote the following to Pestalozzi in May 1803:

> Finally, I am writing you a proper letter, noble friend of man, martyr for humankind, for the good, Columbus of intellectual human education; God willing, crowned with the best crown of human regard, with love of the more noble, the notables, in the Kingdom of God. (Ewald, 1803/2009, p. 596)

Ewald then concluded:

> In short: Christendom is a Pestalozzi method of developing religious concepts, educating a sense of religion, or your method is a Christian method of developing the intellectual abilities—or rather: Both spring forth from the one source, from human nature and its needs. (p. 598)

Pestalozzi enjoyed the role of agent of salvation, and when he took his leave of his staff and pupils to go to Yverdon, he first spoke of Jesus Christ and then said: "When you think of Jesus Christ, so also remember me, in that I have striven to lead you to Him. It is only natural that on this last morning I remind you of what I was to you" (Pestalozzi, 1804/1935, p. 227). A young teacher who was present at the event, Lotte Lutz, wrote afterwards with great enthusiasm to her fiancé and later founder of a Pestalozzi School in Frankfurt, Anton Gruner: "I think that if they crucified him, he would welcome it, for he is Jesus Christ" (Lutz, 1804/1930, p. 1).

7.4 Politics or education?

The numerous advantages of "the Pestalozzi method"—it was natural, simple, holistic, religious, strengthening the person, and applicable without a lot of prior training—made it a popular topic not only in the press but also in the educational administrations of a number of countries. Prussia's interest in the method would be decisive. After Prussia's defeats in Jena and Auerstedt by the forces of Napoleon I (1769–1821) in 1806, it was faced with the task of transforming the state. The idea that change or reorientation should be possible also via a new kind of education had been brought up earlier, but the notion did not achieve a "breakthrough" until 1808, when Fichte, with whom Pestalozzi had discussed the French Revolution in 1793 in Zurich and who was by now a famous philosopher, demanded a new education in his famous series of lectures held in 1807–1808, *Reden an die deutsche Nation* (*Addresses to the German Nation*) and referred to Pestalozzi (Fichte, 1808). It turned out to be very favorable for Pestalozzi that an old friend, Georg Heinrich Ludwig Nicolovius (1767–1839), was Prussian secretary for cultural affairs starting in 1809. Nicolovius worked at first under Wilhelm von Humboldt (1767–1835), who had also developed a liking for "the Pestalozzi method." It is therefore not surprising that Prussia subsequently sent *Eleven*[2] (student teachers) to Pestalozzi to learn the method and then to apply it in their homeland. Most of them had had at least some teaching experience in Prussia and were sent to Yverdon for "further training." They worked as assistant teachers, participating in the life at the institute as teachers and taking care of the children, and now and then they were to send reports back to the relevant parties in Prussia.

After 1803, Prussia and Denmark were the first two countries (after Switzerland) that showed interest in redesigning their education systems to follow the model of "the method." It may be surprising that of all things it was two Lutheran monarchies that showed interest in the educational concept of an avowed republican who in his social ethics was strongly influenced by Zwingli's Reformed Protestantism, who differed considerably from Luther in this area. The decisive point was that "the method" concealed the social ethical implications of Pestalozzi's earlier education, so that it seemed universally employable—that is, it could be applied also in contexts other than republican contexts. The crucial development was reference to the soul of a person, understood as developing naturally, which only lacked the strength to complete the development by itself. Education was help to the soul, and accordingly it had religious as well as cognitive aspirations. No Zwinglian, no Lutheran, and later no Catholic was against the naturalness of the child;[3] no one was against education in accordance with nature in the sense of an unfolding, and many believed with Pestalozzi that this educational and psychological picture of man was the "true" premise of a school and educational method. With Pestalozzi, Europe had found a psychologized educational language that was sufficiently vague to allow for various projections. That is, the promise of the method could be combined with the interest of a national school system and at the same time religion could be safeguarded. The linking of education with a promising future of nation-building belonged to the unquestionable *topos* starting in the years after 1805. It is still the case today.

The question arises as to whether with "the method" Pestalozzi had given up his old republican ideals. He appears to have flirted with this idea, as two letters of September 1805 show. At the beginning of September 1805, Pestalozzi wrote to David Vogel (1760–1849), an old friend from his Zurich days: "I am gripped by melancholy and nostalgia. I am no longer a Zuricher; I am no longer a Swiss. We no longer have a fatherland. Let us remain humans, and let not the interest in humanity in us decrease up to the day we die" (Pestalozzi, 1805/1961a, p. 36). It is not by chance that the passage is reminiscent of Rousseau's introductory passages in *Emile* (Rousseau, 1762/1979), in which Rousseau plays with the idea that in the modern world there is no fatherland and no citizen, which is why a natural person must be educated—an aim, however, that is not met in the novel itself, because in the end Emil is supposed to follow the model of the Roman citizen soldier. Similarly, republicanism shimmers through also in a letter that Pestalozzi wrote in 1805 to his close colleague Johannes Niederer (1779–1843), who was traveling through Switzerland collecting data for a biography of Pestalozzi: "You are now in Zurich. Live with open eyes! Ask especially about the *Lindauer Journal*, in which the Agis essay is printed that is so important to me" (Pestalozzi, 1805/1961b, p. 43).

Politics were not suppressed, but in the signs of the "corrupt" times, they were no longer at the forefront of common good-oriented measures. This central position was given to education, or more precisely, to "the method." For this reason, Pestalozzi wrote the following to Paul Usteri (1768–1831), a well-known Zurich politician, in May 1807: "The dream of making something of people through politics before they really are something—that dream in me has disappeared. My only politics now is to make something of people and to make as much out of people as at all possible" (Pestalozzi, 1807/1961c, p. 251). Political ambition was still a goal, but politics as a means to "leading the people" had largely vanished. Where the appeals to the noble powers also had not resulted in the setting up of their states to the common good of all people—an agenda that had become clear in *Meine Nachforschungen* (Pestalozzi, 1797/1938)—an overall, natural education must make something of people before they can emerge as political beings. Quite evidently, the most various European nations agreed with this program for their national renewal, even though most of them probably had different visions of what a citizen of their state should be.

Notes

1. http://en.wikipedia.org/wiki/Johann_Friedrich_Herbart
2. Teachers that foreign governments sent to Burgdorf and Yverdon to learn "the method" and who were then to return trained in the method to their own countries were called *Eleven*. Regarding the prominence of the political supporters and the number of *Eleven*, Prussia took the lead. The *Eleven* formed their own group, as they were, first, both student teachers and trainees, and, second, did not live in the castle itself but in guest houses. However, there never was any systematic teacher training program, although Pestalozzi had hoped for one.
3. This was a time when the idea of original sin was more understood in a metaphorical way than it was a sincere conviction.

8
European Demands for New Education: Political, National, Private

Abstract: *The all-encompassing educational demand around 1800 in all of Europe directed attention to Pestalozzi. In the five years from 1803 to 1808, an impressive network of interested persons and enthusiasts developed in Europe who saw in "the Pestalozzi method" just the key to the future that they believed that they needed: peaceful, natural, educational, and religious. In the first years, when Pestalozzi was in Burgdorf, the network was limited to German-speaking and French-speaking Switzerland, parts of Germany, and Denmark, where educated circles also spoke German. Closer contacts with Spain started in 1806 and with some French and American philanthropists in 1807. Several educational reform institutes were founded, often under the label "Pestalozzi method."*

Tröhler, Daniel. *Pestalozzi and the Educationalization of the World.* New York: Palgrave Macmillan, 2013.
DOI: 10.1057/9781137346858.

8.1 Pestalozzi and the increasing interest in new educational methods

In 1803, the Act of Mediation issued by Napoleon abolished the Helvetic Republic that had been declared with the invasion of the French troops in 1798. The Act of Mediation, a constitution for a new Swiss confederation, was an attempt at a compromise between the two enemy groups of the supporters and opponents of the Helvetic Revolution. The highly centralized Helvetic Republic was dissolved and the old Swiss federalism reestablished, and a first step towards restoration was made. With the reinstatement of the old cantonal governance structures and administrations, the Burgdorf district governor of Bern wanted to take possession of Burgdorf Castle, where the government offices had always resided prior to the outbreak of the Helvetic Revolution in 1798 but where Pestalozzi's famous institute had been housed in the meantime.

The governor's request caught the conservative government in Bern in a dilemma. It was very clear to the government that for power-symbolic reasons alone the governor had to reside in the castle, but at the same time it also feared public pressure. In October 1803, the government conferred on the future of the castle, and the *Schultheiss* (head of the new-old Bern republic), Niklaus Rudolf von Wattenwyl (1760–1832), proposed the following:

> And if we also look at the very extraordinary sensation that this institute has made in all of Europe, the true raptures that the army of scholars in Germany go into over the advantages of this elementary instruction in all public journals and works, and the danger of entering into a public feud with this intolerant army; consider also that even the French scholars and half-scholars, generals, ministers, etc. have been taken in by it, then also the wisdom of the state enjoins us not to be against the continuation of this institute. (cited in Morf, 1885, p. 15)

However, the local governor in Burgdorf did not relent and gave the government in Bern an ultimatum to either stand with him, the devoted governor of the district, or with Pestalozzi, the favorite of the (former) revolutionary Helvetic Republic. And so, the little council (*Kleiner Rat*) of Bern decided on February 22, 1804 that Pestalozzi must vacate Burgdorf Castle by the fall of 1804 (Kleiner Rat von Bern, 1804/2010, p. 691). News of the decision spread like wildfire, and numerous initiators set about finding a solution for Pestalozzi and his famous institute.

Acting the most quickly was the municipality of Yverdon, located on the southern end of Lake Neuchâtel and with a population of 2,500. On February 14, 1804, even before the little council had made its final decision, Yverdon sent an offer of hospitality to Pestalozzi, proposing that he move his institute to Yverdon Castle (Munizipalität von Yverdon, 1804/2009, p. 688f.). In May 1804, Johann Baptista von Tscharner (1751–1851), patrician and philosopher in Grisons, offered Pestalozzi the use of his own castle in Reichenau (Tscharner, 1804/2009, p. 707),[1] and in June 1804 the city of Payerne offered Pestalozzi their castle as a new home for his educational institute (Munizipalität Payerne, 1804/2009, p. 710f.). Both Yverdon and Payerne were in the French-speaking Canton of Vaud, which had been occupied by Bern from 1536 to 1798 and was now independent. They fought a determined battle to lure Pestalozzi and his institute to their municipalities, while the Canton of Bern tried to interest Pestalozzi in moving his institute to the empty Johanniter monastery in the Bern municipality of Münchenbuchsee.[2]

In the summer of 1804 Pestalozzi decided to move to Yverdon. Accepting the offer by the Canton of Bern, he moved first to the Johanniter monastery in Münchenbuchsee for a few months. He himself stayed in Münchenbuchsee only briefly; he soon moved with his closest staff to Yverdon, where he planned the establishment of the institute and in particular advertised his "method" through publications. When the teachers and pupils followed him to Yverdon in the summer of 1805, Pestalozzi's path to worldwide fame was open. From 1805 to 1820, interest in Pestalozzi spread in Europe and in the United States; it had started shortly after 1800 in parts of Switzerland, in German states, and in Denmark and spread from there in somewhat concentric circles to ever more distant places. Interest in Pestalozzi in England developed only in 1814 after the defeat of Napoleon and thus the end of Napoleon's Continental System (blockade) against the United Kingdom of Great Britain.

8.2 Interest on the part of the political powers

Reception of "the Pestalozzi method" was very early in the Kingdom of Denmark. Already at the close of 1802, King Christian VII (1749–1808) expressed his great interest in a letter to Pestalozzi (König Christian VII, 1802/2009, p. 565f.) and sent two *Eleven* to Burgdorf, Johann Christian

Ludvig Strøm (1771–1859) and Johann Henrich Anton Torlitz (1777–1834). In May 1803 the state school board of the Canton of Lucerne also sent two *Eleven* (Fridolin Kaufmann (1778–1830) and Johann Joseph Eyholzer (1774–1827)) to learn the method (Erziehungsrat Luzern, 1803/2009, p. 593f.). And in July 1803 Pestalozzi received an official letter from the South Prussian Department, a part of Prussia located in Poland today, announcing the arrival of inspector Jospeh Jeziorowski (1767–1856) to learn the method (Südpreussisches Departement, 1803/2009, p. 620). The period in Burgdorf was a breeding ground for the success that would come in the following years in Yverdon.

In the five years from 1803 to 1808, an impressive network of interested persons and enthusiasts developed in Europe who saw in "the Pestalozzi method" just the key to the future that they believed that they needed: peaceful, natural, educational, and religious. In the first years, the network was limited to German-speaking and French-speaking Switzerland, parts of Germany, and Denmark, where educated circles also spoke German. There is evidence of closer contacts with Spain starting in 1806—with Madrilenian Diego López, Herzog von Frias (1754–1811), Joseph Bentura de Caamaño Gayoso Arias Varela et Medoza (1735–1815) of Galicia, and Manuel de Godoy (1767–1851), called the Prince of the Peace of Spain; later, also Franciso Amorós Ondano (1767–1848) joined the ranks of Pestalozzi's admirers. There was interest in France on the part of François Pierre Gauthier Maine de Biran (1766–1824) of Bergerac and in the United States via the two Americans Fulwar Skipwith (1765–1839) and Willam Maclure (1763–1840), who wrote to Pestalozzi from Paris in 1807 expressing their great interest in the method and Skipwith's wish to send his son, Charles, to Pestalozzi for training (Skipwith and Maclure, 1807/2010, p. 261f.); another American interested in Pestalozzi was George Sullivan of Durham, New Hampshire.

These years of Pestalozzi's rise were extremely turbulent in Europe, as they marked the seemingly unstoppable rise of Napoleon, who for Pestalozzi was both a blessing and a curse. In the spring of 1807, when Spain discovered Pestalozzi during the course of the Napoleonic reign in Europe, Spain had to supply France with 15,000 soldiers for the conquest of East Prussia and Russia. Godoy, who was a statesman and lieutenant-general, had to flee Spain forever together with King Charles IV and the king's wife, Maria Luisa of Parma, in the summer of 1808 after domestic riots and a popular revolt. This put an early end to Spanish efforts to introduce (in a very local and small way) "the Pestalozzi method" (to replace King Charles IV, Napoleon installed his oldest brother, Joseph Bonaparte, as King Joseph I of Spain).[3] But in the spring of 1808, before the fate of the Pestalozzi method on the Iberian Peninsula was sealed, the southern German kingdom of Württemberg, where King Friedrich I (1754–1816) had been installed by Napoleon in 1806, began to show interest in Pestalozzi. This interest sent a powerful signal.

A short time later, in September 1808, the home secretary of Holland, Frederik Auguste van Leyden (1768–1821), acting for the king (another brother of Napoleon's who was made King of Holland in 1806 (Louis Napoleon Bonaparte (1778–184)), contacted Pestalozzi concerning implementing "the method" in specific Dutch educational institutes (Leyden, 1808/2010, p. 546f.). In addition, in November 1808 Friedrich August, Duke of Nassau-Usingen (1738–1816) contacted Pestalozzi about introducing the method throughout his duchy, where Nassau-Usingen, like Württemberg, was part of the anti-Prussian Confederation of the Rhine[4] formed by Napoleon. A few weeks previously, Prussia, shaken by its losses against Napoleon, had asked Pestalozzi, in the name of King Frederick William III, to help build the education system. First, Friedrich Leopold von Schrötter (1743–1815), an aristocrat and Prussian statesman, asked Pestalozzi whether Prussian *Eleven* could be sent to Yverdon (Schrötter, 1808/2010, p. 540), and later Nicolovius a high official and Pestalozzi friend, wrote to Pestalozzi (Nicolovius, 1808/2010, p. 552 f). And in May 1809, Wilhelm von Humboldt (1767–1835), head of the culture and education section at the Prussian ministry of the interior, and Johann Wilhelm von Süvern (1775–1829) wrote personally to Pestalozzi to organize the further systematic sending of Prussian *Eleven* to Yverdon (Sektion Unterricht des preussischen Innenministerium, 1809/2010a, p. 691, 2010b, p. 744f.): given the importance of Prussia, this commission to train Prussian teacher-educators in "the method" amounted to a knightly accolade in the area of education policy.

8.3 Interest on the part of activists and concerned parents

There is a certain irony in the fact that precisely monarchic power-holders in Europe were interested in a method of education that had been "discovered" by a republican advocate and propagated by a republican government. This was connected, for one, with the fact that Pestalozzi's method was supposedly based purely on the natural development of the child and thus was seemingly context-free in design and could be implemented in any context. For another, around 1800, especially in Protestant regions of Europe, the educationalization of social problems described at the beginning of this book became visible and resulted in massive publications and intensive educational and experimental and reform activity. The issue was not yet the introduction of an elaborated schoopl system functioning according to meritocratic principles—that would become possible only after the end of Napoleon's reign in the nation-states legitimized by constitutions—but rather popular education—that is, the systematic education of the (lower) classes.

There was no systematic teacher education at the time. Committed contemporaries published educational journals that were intended to be helpful to teachers. Most of these journals were published by Protestant theologians or sons of pastors. Typical of the period, although early, was the *Taschenbuch für teutsche Schulmeister* [Pocketbook for German Teachers],[5] published by a Protestant pastor named Christoph Ferdinand Moser starting in 1786. Moser (1793) wrote that the pocketbook contained "means by which a school master who has learned no profession can still behave in a respectable way even when he has a low income" (p. 237). Moser strongly recommended that teachers did not engage in other work alongside teaching, as that would "degrade both your office and your own person too much" (p. 237 f.). Here he meant night watchman work, keeping watch over cattle, harvesting, threshing, wood splitting, or woodworking—all being jobs that "wither not only the body but also the powers of the soul" (p. 238). Moser made 18 suggestions for dealing with an excessively low income. First, the teacher should choose "a sensible and industrious wife" who is "not without means and who has a good reputation"; second, he himself should be very frugal; third, he should win the trust of the authorities, superiors, parents, and children and raise his own children to be industrious early on. If he needed a sideline job, he should teach private lessons, repair church or parlor clocks, or work in the wine trade; if he lived in a wine region, he could deal in writing materials, seeds, soap, or lard, without competing with the local grocers and not purely for profit, so as to ensure the "well-being of his soul" (p. 239–242).

Towards 1800, when the periodical was discontinued (in 1797), Moser's *Taschenbuch* was very commonplace, and the number of educational publications was enormous. Just how vast the educational literature was is described by Johann Christoph Friedrich GutsMuths (1759–1839),[6] a Protestant theologian, upper secondary school teacher, and geography teacher at the Schnepfenthal School, in the pilot issue in 1800 of his journal, *Bibliothek der pädagogischen Literatur* [Library of the Educational Literature], one of the first review journals. GutsMuths wrote that the purpose of his journal was to announce valuable works and to also discuss the most important works of the 300 to 500 publications on education published annually in Germany alone (GutsMuths, 1800, p. 1f.). Upon this background, academic reflection on education developed that called itself *Erziehungswissenschaft* [educational science]. In 1803 in *Beiträge zur Erziehungskunst* [Contributions to the Art of Education], a journal published by Christian Weiss (1774–1853) (son of a pastor and philosopher and theologian trained in German Kantianism) and Ernst Tillich (1780–1867) (son of a teacher and also a Kantian philosopher), Weiss wrote that he envied anyone "who put his own strengths...into an occupation where he helps thousands of individuals, noticeably reduces the total misery among humankind, and can noticeably increase the total welfare" (Weiss, 1803, p. 2f.); the only thing that was still needed was an educational science that would successfully aid this "most momentous and venerable" art (p. 5, p 8f.).

In the wake of these currents, the emergence of which had nothing to do with Pestalozzi, attention turned to Pestalozzi, who had public support and promised publicly that with his method the practical problems of a world in the grips of educationalization could be solved, taking nature as a reference, starting with loving mothers in the home, and resulting in religiousness. Many of the supporters of this educational turn had themselves founded educational reform institutions that have largely not been examined—studied empirically and interpreted culturally—up to today.[7] Quite a few of them called themselves Pestalozzi or Pestalozzian schools in order to compete successfully on the market (Horlacher, 2011, 2013). Many of them asked Pestalozzi to send experts when they set up their educational institutes, such as a Prussian lawyer, Wilhelm Christian von Türk (1774–1846), who was appointed to oversee the school system in 1801 and made an education trip to the most well-known educational institutes of the day in Germany and Switzerland. After completing his trip, he asked Pestalozzi to send him an expert: "You give me one of your pupils as an assistant, and in this way, the seeds of human welfare will be sown also in the north and bring forth a rich harvest" (Türk, 1805/2010, p. 13ff.). But as Pestalozzi himself did not have enough members of staff, von Türk traveled to Yverdon in 1807, where he stayed until 1811. From Yverdon he also made a successful effort to win over Frederick William III (1770–1840), King of Prussia, for the implementation of "the Pestalozzi method."

Most of the Pestalozzi propagandists were from this socially committed, mostly Protestant, milieu and they paved the way for him to the highest government authorities. An example is the now forgotten Protestant theologian Johann Ernst Plamann (1771–1834)[8] from Rzepczyno (in West Pomerania). After teaching in the home of his brother-in-law, Plamann completed the examination required for a job as preacher and then started teaching in 1797 at an institute for the sons of educated families. In 1802 the poet Christoph August Tiedge (1752–1841)[9] advised him to read the works of Pestalozzi. Delighted by Pestalozzi's books and the propaganda, Plamann traveled to Burgdorf in 1803 and stayed for half a year. Pestalozzi wanted Plamann to stay and work at the institute, but Plamann, apparently already engaged to be married, returned to Berlin. In the same year, Plamann received royal permission to found his own institute, which he opened together with Johann Marius Friedrich Schmidt (1776–1849) in September 1805 (Plamann, 1805a). Lacking trained teaching staff, Plamann turned to Pestalozzi for help, who sent him an assistant from Switzerland, Johannes Preisig (1775–1814).[10] Plamann published a number of works on the Pestalozzi method (Plamann, 1805b, 1806, 1812/1815), and he became, together with von Türk who was in Yverdon, the center point for everyone in the Prussian state who was interested in the method. In Berlin he was also, together with Pestalozzi's friend Nicolovius in the ministry of the interior, the interface between Yverdon and Prussia.[11]

8.4 Pestalozzi and the rise of a wide educational public

Plamann's Pestalozzian school for boys, founded in 1805, was just one of the many schools established under the Pestalozzi label.[12] These institutes, which were often very short-lived, bear witness to a growing market of education-conscious parents. Whereas wealthy parents tended to stick to the model of the private tutor and educated their children at home and the parents of poor families became integrated in the growing system of mass education, for families between poverty and aristocracy there was an institutional gap. The innumerable private institutes that emerged after 1800 bear witness to the large and ever-increasing demands of well-off parents who were willing to pay for their children's education. They had understood the message of modern times and identified comprehensive education as an indispensable foundation for their children's success—all that was (yet) missing were the public institutions that would be established only after the founding of the constitutional nation-states.

An example here is Johann Rudolf Marti (1765–1824), a very wealthy businessman from Glarus in Switzerland who lived in Riga in East Prussia. At the end of 1800 Marti married his second wife, Gertrud Helena Schmid (1771–1809) from Pärnu (in Estonia), who had three sons from a previous marriage. To give the boys a good education, Marti contacted Pestalozzi in September 1803, wanting to hand over "my three sons to you for instruction and to place them completely under your fatherly direction" (Marti, 1803/2009, p. 649). Having a similar interest was Georges de Rougemont (1758–1824), who was a general public prosecutor, politician, and senior military officer in Neuchâtel. He contacted Pestalozzi in May 1808 and asked him to accept as a pupil his son, Georges de Rougemont (1802–1810) (de Rougemont, 1808/2010, p. 478). And dozens of other parents in Switzerland and abroad had the same interest as well.

Very wealthy families sent their children's teachers to Yverdon along with their children. Baden's minister of finance and councilor, Georg Heinrich Ferdinand Vierordt (1758–1823), and Christian Friedrich Meerwein (1770–1843), a merchant in Carlsruhe, sent their sons Heinrich Vierordt (1797–1867) and Karl Friedrich Meerwein (1800–1814) to Yverdon with garrison school teacher Johann Georg König (1781–1842), who lived with them in the castle (Ladomus, 1808/2010, p. 487f.). The most famous of these teachers accompanying their charges was certainly Friedrich Wilhelm August Fröbel (in English often Froebel) (1782–1852),[13] who—after having visited Yverdon briefly in 1805—asked Pestalozzi to admit his three charges and himself in July 1808 and spent the years from 1808 to 1811 together with the three sons of the noble von Holzhausen family of Frankfurt[14] at Pestalozzi's institute in Yverdon (Fröbel, 1808, p. 507ff.). Through Fröbel another connection with Germany was made—namely, with Franz Adam Lejeune (1765–1854), a physician who treated a number of wealthy citizens and members of aristocratic families and who, at Fröbel's suggestion, visited Pestalozzi in Yverdon in 1806. In 1808 Lejeune sent his two sons to Yverdon for four years.[15]

At the end of the first decade of the nineteenth century, still during Napoleon's reign in Europe, an educationalized public of power holders, activists, and ambitious parents had been formed that focused particularly strongly on Pestalozzi, who for his part never tired of further reinforcing their expectations. In 1809 Pestalozzi was at his zenith—165 pupils as well as 63 teachers and interns were at the institute in Yverdon.

Notes

1. Pestalozzi declined Tscharner's offer on May 20, 1804, citing distance as his main reason (Pestalozzi, 1804/1951, p. 199f.).
2. Many of Pestalozzi's staff favored the idea of moving to close-by Münchenbuchsee. The plan was to enter into close cooperation with another famous educator and reformer, Philipp Emanuel von Fellenberg (1771–1834) (http://en.wikipedia.org/wiki/Philipp_Emanuel_von_Fellenberg). Von Fellenberg had his own famous educational institute very close by, and the plan was for Fellenberg to take over the administrative management, while Pestalozzi could devote himself more to research and writing. The plan failed, not least due to differences in their ideas on how the institute could be run.
3. Interest in Pestalozzi in Spain can be largely traced back to Swiss mercenaries who served in Spain's army as senior officers. The "Regiment-School," set up following "the Pestalozzi method" was founded in the fall of 1803 by Colonel Ludwig von Wimpfen (1765-1831), and a Swiss captain, Franz Joseph Stephan Voitel (1773–1839), was put in charge. Twenty to 30 children of members of the regiment were taught; later, the school opened its doors to the children of Madrid's leading families.
4. The Confederation of the Rhine was a confederation of initially 16 client states of the First French Empire under the rule of Napoleon, after Napoleon defeated Austria's Francis II (1768–1835) and Russia's Alexander I (1777–1825) in the Battle of Austerlitz. It lasted from 1806 to 1813. http://en.wikipedia.org/wiki/Confederation_of_the_Rhine
5. The entire journal is available online at http://goobiweb.bbf.dipf.de/viewer/toc/ZDB025285408/0/LOG_0000/
6. https://en.wikipedia.org/wiki/Johann_Christoph_Friedrich_GutsMuths
7. An exception is Scholz (2011) on school reforms and teacher education in Brandenburg-Prussia or Godenzi (2012) on private schools in the Canton of Zurich from 1800 to 1820.
8. http://en.wikipedia.org/wiki/Johann_Ernst_Plamann
9. http://en.wikipedia.org/wiki/Christoph_August_Tiedge

European Demands for New Education   93

10 Johannes Preisig (1775–1814) of Gais (Canton of Appenzell-Ausserrhoden) is a very typical nameless representative of this educational turn. In Burgdorf and Yverdon, Preisig was one of the adults who had entered the institute to learn the method. There are gaps in the available information on his life: in 1805 he was recommended to Plamann and probably went to Berlin; and in 1812 he was again in Yverdon with Pestalozzi and in the same year was a mining-inspector in Reichenau (Canton of Grisons). He died in 1814.

11 In 1812 Plamann gave up his institute and traveled again to Pestalozzi in Yverdon. Upon his next return to Germany to set up an institute that existed until 1827, he acquired a house in Berlin.

12 Another, and a very typical, example is Johannes de L'Aspée (1783–1825), who completed training and further training during several stays in Yverdon. After receiving approval from the government of the Duchy of Nassau to set up an elementary school following Pestalozzi's principles in 1808, he opened a private educational institute for boys in Wiesbaden in 1809 that stood in competition with the state schools; it was expanded to become a boarding school in 1814. In 1810 and 1814 L'Aspée held public examinations at his institute and at the event presented the Pestalozzi method to visitors. One of L'Aspée's papers on Pestalozzi was translated into English (de L'Aspée, 1865).

13 After discontinuing his studies in mathematics/natural sciences in Jena (from 1799 to 1801) and working at some forestry jobs, Fröbel began teaching in 1805 at the Pestalozzi Model School in Frankfurt founded by Wilhelm Friedrich Hufnagel (1754–1830), a Protestant theologian (see Horlacher, 2011). Gottlieb Anton Gruner joined the school somewhat later, when the school was in difficulties and sought to be successful again under the Pestalozzi label. After Fröbel returned from Yverdon and after further studies in Göttingen (1811) and Berlin (1812), voluntary service (1813–1814) in the wars of liberation against Napoleon, and a job as an assistant at the Museum of Mineralogy in Berlin, he founded the *Allgemeine Deutsche Erziehungsanstalt* [universal German educational institute] in Griesheim (Thüringen) in 1816. He moved the institute to Keilhau in 1817. Due to the unconventional (for the times) educational elements practiced and tested there, Fröbel was accused of demagoguery. The institute was in difficulties when Fröbel left it in 1831. He founded an educational institute in Wartensee (Lucerne), Switzerland, which was moved to Willisau and then closed shortly afterwards. In 1834 he received an appointment by the government of Bern in Burgdorf, where he taught teacher education courses, and from 1835 to 1836 he headed the orphanage in Burgdorf (Bern) but found himself the object of public criticism and hostility. After returning to Germany, Fröbel devoted himself almost exclusively to the education of preschool-age children, both practically and theoretically. Central to his educational concept was his opinion that children should be stimulated and guided in all aspects by

planned age-appropriate, physical and mental play activities, sayings, and songs, and always close to nature. The idea of the kindergarten met with great approval, but in 1851 the culture and education section at the Prussian ministry of the interior banned kindergartens on the grounds of their alleged destructive potential in the areas of religion and politics. The ban was lifted in 1860.

14 Carl (Anton Friedrich Wilhelm August Rudolf) von Holzhausen (1794–1867), Friedrich (Ludwig Carl) von Holzhausen (1797–1819), and (Johann) Adolph von Holzhausen (1799–1861).

15 August Eduard Lejeune (1797–1882) and Johann Gustav Adolf Lejeune (1800–1880).

9
Pestalozzi's Charisma, a Guarantee of Success and a Problem

Abstract: *Due to political unrest Pestalozzi moved his institute from Burgdorf to Yverdon in the French part of Switzerland. The European interest grew on the part of neighboring countries and on the part of families that wanted to give their children the best possible education and saw promise in Pestalozzi's institute. The success of the first years of the institute in Yverdon is illustrated clearly by the numbers: in 1805 there were only about 20 pupils at the school. But in 1806–1807 there were already 80, by 1808 there were 134, and in 1809 enrollment peaked at 165. Internal conflicts—especially organizational problems—in the institute were suppressed by Pestalozzi's charisma, but they were not solved. When the German philosopher Fichte praised Pestalozzi's method as starting point of a new age in his* Addresses to the German Nation *delivered in 1808, all the internal problems were forgotten for a while.*

Tröhler, Daniel. *Pestalozzi and the Educationalization of the World.* New York: Palgrave Macmillan, 2013.
DOI: 10.1057/9781137346858.

9.1 Growth and success

The institute in the castle of Yverdon was not officially opened until 1805, which had given Pestalozzi the opportunity to continue to write, and he once again took up the topic of education of the poor and vocational education. However, this was not something that he could implement in his institute as, for one, the institute was for "elementary education" and, for another, the clientele was from ever "better" families and did not require vocational education in the sense of education for the underprivileged. Pestalozzi's plans and considerations—outlined in *Zweck und Plan einer Armen-Erziehungs-Anstalt* [Purpose and Plan for an Educational Institute for the Poor] (Pestalozzi, 1805/1943a), *Aufruf für die Armenanstalt* [Appeal for an Institute for the Poor] (Pestalozzi, 1805/1943b), *Über Volksbildung und Industrie* [On Popular Education and Industry] (Pestalozzi, 1806/1943c), and *Ein Gespräch über Volksaufklärung und Volksbildung* [A Conversation about Enlightenment and Education of the Poor] (Pestalozzi, 1806/1943d) and all written in 1805 and 1806—were never published. They remained (for the time being) ideas and ideals and thus unfulfilled hope.

But interest in "the method" grew on the part of neighboring countries (initially northern countries) and on the part of families that wanted to give their children the best possible education and saw promise in Pestalozzi's institute. The success in the first years of the institute in Yverdon is illustrated clearly by the numbers: in 1805 there were only about 20 pupils at the school. But in 1806–1807 there were already 80, by 1808 there were 134, and in 1809 enrollment peaked at 165. The number of teachers also rose correspondingly: in 1807 there were 20 teachers; within two years the number rose by 50 % to 31. This does not include the number of *Eleven*, trainees sent to Pestalozzi to learn "the method," which fluctuated between 10 and 30. In 1809, then, there were over 200 people in the neat castle at Yverdon with Pestalozzi, the "father" of the institute and now 63 years old. In the 20 years of the Yverdon institute's existence (from 1805 to 1825), we can reconstruct that there was a total of 920 pupils and 335 teachers and assistant teachers.

As a result of the large number of people at the institute, the burden of the high expectations coming from the outside, and in part difficult personnel management within the institute, Pestalozzi himself seldom taught. But for the pupils and the teachers, school lessons were the main activity. According to the school timetable from the early years at

Yverdon, the pupils had ten hours of instruction daily, six days per week, from six in the morning until eight in the evening, with a two-hour break at midday that included a walk. A quantitative analysis of the 60 hours of school lessons per week for all six classes/grades reveals the following breakdown of school subjects:

- Languages (German, French, and (in grade 6) Latin) 45%
- Arithmetic and geometry 25%
- Singing/drawing 15%
- Religion 6%
- Geography 5%
- History 2%
- Natural history 1%

Lessons thus dominated life at the institute. Instruction was divided into school subjects and taught in clearly defined time units, and the pupils were assigned to classes according to individual performance and subject. The data show that "the shaping of the whole human character" that had been publicized turned out to be a relatively normal school program, but it was also complemented by regular moral and religious speeches that Pestalozzi gave to pupils and teachers. Physical education consisted in daily walks and also in republican militia-style drills in the institute's own little cadet battalion. The battalion had a flag (see following page) that provides some information on the unity that Pestalozzi always propagated, which was expressed in the life of the institute as corporate identity with Pestalozzi as the sole integrating figure. The flag had an emblematic design inscribed with a single name, "Pestalozzi," and pictured Winkelried,[1] the legendary hero of the Battle of Sempach in 1368[2] who had brought about the victory of the Swiss Confederacy, sacrificing his life by throwing himself upon the pikes of the enemy Habsburg army to break up their ranks. The motto on the flag, "*in amore virtus*," creates a connection with the republican ideal citizen, and the emblem also depicts a (republican) line from Winkelried to Pestalozzi, making a reference to salvation through sacrifice.

Personnel management at Yverdon was organized correspondingly paternalistically. Pestalozzi interpreted problems among the staff members mostly as doubt concerning the institute and thus concerning the head of the institute. Pestalozzi had no qualms about responding to conflicts by staging grotesque scenes. For instance, on New Year's Day in 1808, he appeared before a convening of the pupils and teachers with

Pestalozzi flag in Yverdon.

a coffin and a skull supposedly belonging to a friend who had recently died, and said:

> See here her skull. - - - See here my coffin. What remains for me? The hope of my grave. My heart is in shreds. I am no longer what I was yesterday. I no longer have the love that I enjoyed yesterday. I no longer have the trust that I had yesterday. Why should I live on? (Pestalozzi, 1808/1964a, p. 3)

Pestalozzi did live on—for another 17 years, in fact, but using these means he did not succeed in keeping the institute together in the long run.

9.2   Internal conflicts and problems

The success of "the Pestalozzi method" in these years in Europe was unparalleled, and it was due, among other things, to Pestalozzi's charisma, which had a very convincing effect on his contemporaries. However, for the head of an institute charisma is not sufficient, and Yverdon was not spared conflicts.

A serious conflict occurred in 1808–1809, at the time when Pestalozzi was having his greatest success. The conflict became apparent on September 20, 1808, when Pestalozzi received two letters from teachers at the institute: one from Johannes Niederer in the name of several of the teachers (Niederer, 1808/2010) and the other from Hermann Krüsi (Krüsi, 1808/2010). Niederer's letter announced, first, that they refused to help with organization and direction of the institute and that they wanted to focus solely on teaching school subjects and, second, that he, Niederer, was giving Pestalozzi notice that he would soon be leaving the institute. Krüsi's letter was a letter of resignation, in which he took his leave of the life of the institute. In his letter, Niederer recalled what Pestalozzi had been to him, and his memories are a good illustration of the exaggerated ambitions that had been developed in Yverdon in those months when it was receiving great interest in Europe. Niederer wrote that he had once seen in Pestalozzi "the image of man transfigured by God" and, clearer still, "in you Jesus Christ was revealed to me. No, that was no deception that I saw" (Niederer, 1808/2010, p. 555). However, the "Pestalozzi the mortal" had not really grasped all that he, Niederer, was capable of, and Niederer had therefore been employed merely according to the yardstick of "the material exigencies of the material side of the existing house," meaning the institute in Yverdon. Niederer was not satisfied with his role there, which was the role of religion teacher, and he did not want the task to which he had been assigned, that of developing religious instruction. What he apparently had in mind for himself was to be a further developer and messenger of "the method" rather than to waste his time developing a school subject (in his case, religion). He stated explicitly that he was no longer willing to be involved in the supervision of one school subject or other at the institute (p. 555).

Just shortly before this, in September 1808, Pestalozzi had made a plea to his staff to take on such tasks and other supervisory activities. He held a speech at the institute titled *Über die Aufsicht* [On Supervision] (Pestalozzi, 1808/1964b) that shows clearly that he expected the staff to participate more in the overall organization of the institute and not simply teach their school subjects. In caring for the children also outside of the lessons the task was not to guide the children towards "outer endurance in performing their duties" but rather to strengthen them "in their will to develop a general will for the good," upon which the success of the method was based. For this reason, Pestalozzi stated, he also wanted the teachers to attend the morning devotions held by Pestalozzi, so that when supervising the children during the day they could refer back to the content of the moral lessons of the morning. He also wanted the teachers to attend his Sunday observances. In addition, he wanted religious instruction to be developed and organized with regard to the fundamental aim—the success of the method (Pestalozzi, 1808/1964b, p. 207f.).

Niederer, who had resided for a year outside the institute and came to the castle mainly to teach religion and to attend teacher conferences, felt—quite rightly— personally affected by this. But his letter to Pestalozzi expresses more than only personal consternation concerning the practical overall organization of the institute; it also reveals his fundamental theoretical differences with Pestalozzi. In the part of his letter in which he terminates his editing work for Pestalozzi's periodical *Wochenschrift für Menschenbildung* [Weekly Journal for Human Education], in publication since 1807, Niederer (1808/2010) wrote:

> The *Wochenschrift* can hardly be continued by me, since, for example, in my answer to Fichte on the topic of language I would have to say exactly the opposite of what you said at the assembly. I cannot impose my principles upon the public as yours, even if they arise directly from your ideas, where they directly contradict them. (p. 556)

This passage is extremely informative, because it points to the above-mentioned expectations in a Europe dominated by Napoleon and to the interpretations of "the Pestalozzi method." For Niederer was asserting nothing less than that he was a better interpreter of the method than Pestalozzi was. In this context he mentioned the German philosopher Fichte, who had commented on Pestalozzi in a publication. Specifically, he was referring to Fichte's *Reden an die Deutsche Nation* (*Addresses to the German Nation*) (Fichte 1808, 1808/2008), a series of speeches delivered by Fichte in the winter of 1807–1808 and in which the Pestalozzi method is praised as central means for a complete renewal of mankind.

9.3 Fichte's *Addresses to the German Nation* (1808)

Fichte's *Addresses to the German Nation* are extraordinarily important for an understanding of the time, for they reflect, for one, the end of the

800-year-old Holy Roman Empire of the German Nation (by the French army's defeat of the Prussian troops in 1805 and 1806) and, for another, the philosophical breakthrough of German nationalism, which would last for far more than a century and often referred to Fichte. And not least, the *Addresses* elevated education to the principal means of saving the nation and the future of humankind, while making Pestalozzi the chief witness. The collapse of the Holy Roman Empire of the German Nation was extremely important from a European perspective, because the individual German states could hardly defend themselves against the French army. The German Nation was shaken by Napoleon's victory over Austria and Russia at the Battle of Austerlitz on December 2, 1805, and it was shattered once and for all in 1806 when Napoleon dissolved the Holy Roman Empire of the German Nation and established the Confederation of the Rhine (with Napoleon as its "protector") with the now sovereign states of Bavaria, Württemberg, and Baden. These states, which consequently underwent an extensive process of modernization, supplied Napoleon with large numbers of military personnel for his further conquests in Spain and eastern Europe. On October 14, 1806 the Prussians and Saxons were defeated in the twin battles of Jena and Auerstedt, and two weeks later French troops occupied Berlin. With the Treaty of Tilsit in July 1807, the Kingdom of Prussia surrendered to France, and Prussia was reduced to half of its former size. As a result, comprehensive democratic reforms were implemented in Prussia. The first free elections for wealthy citizens were held in 1809, and as a part of education reforms the University of Berlin (today Humboldt-Universität zu Berlin) was founded in 1810. The first vice chancellor of the university and rector from 1811 to 1812 was Fichte, who in *Addresses* (Fichte, 1808/2008) had protested against the humiliation of Germany by the French, propagated the idea of the German nation, and in that connection also highlighted "the Pestalozzi method." The passage with Fichte's comments on Pestalozzi was printed in the fall of 1808 in Pestalozzi's *Wochenschrift für Menschenbildung* (issues 11 to 14) along with an unfinished commentary by Niederer.

Fichte interpreted the events in Austerlitz, Jena, Auerstedt, and Tilsit as the high point of an epoch in history that represented the "State of Complete Sinfulness" (Fichte, 1808/2008, p. xx). But with this high point, Fichte saw the possibility of a new beginning, the threshold of a new era, the starting point of which was to be the *Addresses*—and thus also the Pestalozzi method. It was to be nothing less than the spiritual and moral new establishment of the Holy Roman Empire of the German Nation to save the whole world, or at least Europe. Already in the first of the 14 addresses, which Fichte delivered at the Berlin Academy in the winter of 1807–1808, he proposed "the complete reform of the current educational system as the only means of preserving the existence of the German nation" (Fichte, 1808/2008, p. 17); this would be distinctly different than the old education that fostered human selfishness. Fichte submitted that the "art of education such as we desire has in reality already been invented and is being practiced" (p. 19), but rather than reveal to whom he was referring, he examined in detail the characteristics of this new education in the Second Address. The new education would consist in a mental/intellectual part, which should give the young person an image, a pre-figuration of the good life, and an emotional part, which should give the person the strength and passion to put all these mental images into action (p. 24f.). However, the mental education, the mental activity of forming images for life, should not (and this shows Fichte's idealism) take place in the empirical world but rather in the philosophical ideal world:

> This [mental] education is therefore in its final consequence the cultivation of the pupil's faculty of cognition, and on no account an historical schooling in the permanent qualities of things, but the higher and philosophical schooling in the [pure] laws according to which such a permanent quality of things becomes necessary. (p. 26)

Accordingly, love should not be sensuous but rather religious and moral (p. 30f.), and for this the pupil should be "brought completely and uninterruptedly under the influence of this education," entirely separated from the spoiled world, "separated from the community and kept safe from any contact with it" (p. 31; see also p. 32).

Fichte (1808/2008) continued his description of the new education in the Third Address and explained in the fourth through eighth addresses why such a comprehensive change could take place exclusively in Germany. His main argument was that only the German language had remained an unadulterated language, and that for this reason it was easier for Germans to discover mental truths or original images, whereas other languages—Fichte means French but does not say so explicitly—stemmed from the dead language of Latin and had less potential (pp. 57–58.). The importance of the power of the original German language had been made clear by Luther, a "leader inspired by the eternal" (p. 75). In Luther it had become apparent that the Germans should be viewed "as a people, an original people, the people as such" (p. 96), in which lay the "law of the development of the original and divine" (p. 103), if young people received the correct education. And then Fichte put forward the positive news: this type of education, which would save the German people from the decline due to the French occupation and which would be to the benefit of the whole world, already existed in the real world—namely: "It shall proceed from the course of instruction devised and proposed by Johann Heinrich Pestalozzi, and already successfully put into practice under his supervision" (p. 119). Fichte compared Pestalozzi to Luther, as both were examples of the characteristics of the German soul (p, 119), standing out with their "almighty love" (p. 120), the "achievements of which far surpassed even his [Pestalozzi's] hopes" (p. 120):

> He wanted merely to help the people; but his discovery, when its full implications are taken into consideration, exalts the people, abolishes all differences between them and the cultivated class, provides, instead of the popular education he envisaged, a national education. (p. 120)

Like Niederer at the same time point in Yverdon, Fichte believed that he recognized far more in Pestalozzi than Pestalozzi himself could ever have been aware of. Fichte's certainty that he recognized the essence of "the Pestalozzi method" led him to criticize some of the executions of the method, such as, namely, the learning of language (Fichte, 1808/2008, p. 123). Pestalozzi wanted to anchor language acquisition to the sense impressions, specifically to the naming of the child's body parts, which for him was the principle of the natural in education but for Fichte was "completely misguided" (p. 124). Fichte stated that Pestalozzi "proceeds from the perfectly correct proposition that that first object of the child's knowledge must be the child himself" (p. 124), "but is the body of the child then the child himself?" (p. 124)—an unbearable idea for a German idealist.

9.4 Education policy interest in "the method"

As it became clear above, Niederer agreed with Fichte's criticism of Pestalozzi's language education, and he refused to continue his work on the weekly journal *Wochenschrift für Menschenbildung*. In 1808, the *Wochenschrift für Menschenbildung* printed the three addresses by Fichte that discussed Pestalozzi, along with the unfinished commentary by Niederer that remained unspecific. Niederer followed through on his letter of September 20, 1808 only in part: whereas he never completed his commentary on Fichte, he also did not leave the institute in Yverdon (nor did Krüsi). The reason for this change of heart is unknown, but it may have been connected with the concrete education-policy importance of the Pestalozzi method for Prussia and its uncertain future.

Namely, just a few days after receiving the letters from Niederer and Krüsi, Pestalozzi received a letter from his Prussian friend Nicolovius (1808/2010), who in August 1808 had written a formal note to the king of Prussia introducing "a better method in the elementary schools" (*Einführung einer bessern Methode in die Elementarschulen betreffend*), bringing Pestalozzi into play. Enclosed with the letter from Nicolovius was a letter from Schrötter (1808/2010), who was the minister of education in Prussia. In the name of the Prussian king Schrötter asked what would be required of any future *Eleven* sent to Yverdon by Prussia to learn "the Pestalozzi method" for application in Prussia. Only a few days later, Pestalozzi received a letter from the famous historian Johannes von Müller, who had been appointed state minister of education in Westphalia (a member of the Confederation of the Rhine) by Napoleon one year earlier and who was also inquiring about practical implementation of the method. And just four weeks later, on November 1, 1808, a letter arrived in Yverdon from the newly founded Duchy of Nassau (also a member of the Confederation of the Rhine) inquiring about assistance with reforming the education sector (Lehr, 1808/2010, pp. 600–601). The revolution exported from France had clearly created in Europe undreamed of demand among education policymakers (apart from all the interest on the part of private individuals) that probably led to a glossing over of the internal differences at Yverdon. And whereas the internal conflicts settled down, they were not resolved. One year later, in the spring of 1810, when the method was criticized publicly for the first time, the internal conflicts immediately broke out again. They caused the more or less steady (although not linear) downfall of the institute ending in the year 1825.

Notes

1. http://en.wikipedia.org/wiki/Arnold_von_Winkelried
2. http://en.wikipedia.org/wiki/Battle_of_Sempach

10
Public Critique, Restoration, Pestalozzi's Lonesome End, and the Beginning of Modern Mass Education

Abstract: *An official state evaluation of the Pestalozzi method in Yverdon in 1810 judged that the method practiced at the institute was appropriate for a family-type educational institution but would not serve as a model for mass schooling in a modern state. This sobering report caused the tensions to escalate, and years of ups and downs were ahead of Pestalozzi. After Napoleon's end and the Congress of Vienna (1814–1815) Switzerland was in danger of being divided between France (in Restoration) and conservative Austria. This triggered Pestalozzi's writing of his political testament. The devastating economic crises of 1816–1817 reminded him of his original vocation, education for the poor, which reinforced the problems in Yverdon.*

Tröhler, Daniel. *Pestalozzi and the Educationalization of the World*. New York: Palgrave Macmillan, 2013.
DOI: 10.1057/9781137346858.

10.1 Pestalozzi's fight in vain for official recognition in Switzerland

The years from 1808 to 1810 brought Pestalozzi great fame among many governmental authorities, mainly in the numerous German monarchies. The high point was the official interest on the part of the Kingdom of Prussia, which led Pestalozzi to receive greater recognition also in Switzerland. Some cantons of Switzerland had requested information on "the method," but as a rule the Swiss interest came from private persons or local school boards, such as the school board of Kreuzlingen in the Canton of Thurgau. However, there was no official recognition of "the method's" potential. There was astonishment in Yverdon in the summer of 1809 when the Swiss Confederate Legislative Assembly awarded a public commendation to Philipp Emanuel von Fellenberg,[1] who had been Pestalozzi's rival in educational questions for many years. Von Fellenberg was commended for his agricultural innovations, which had been very welcome in the time of the Napoleon's Continental Blockade with its terrible consequences for Switzerland's proto-industry. Somewhat hurt by the official recognition of his old rival, on June 20, 1809 Pestalozzi asked Ludwig d'Affry, who was head of the Canton of Fribourg and at the same time elected Head of the Confederation, to conduct an official state evaluation of the importance of "the method" for Switzerland, specifically for an evaluation of the question as to "whether the principles and means of the method grant the fatherland important benefits and through what prescribed orders these benefits could be realized for the fatherland" (Pestalozzi, 1809/1964c, p. 274).

With this, Pestalozzi was aiming for universal implementation of his method in Swiss schools. Just how important this national recognition was to him is shown by a second letter that he wrote to d'Affry shortly after (Pestalozzi, 1809/1964d). In close resemblance with most of the descriptions of him, Pestalozzi's letter referred to the "difficult course of my life" and elucidated that evaluation of the institute made true sense only if one knew the "reach," the "depth," and the "means" of "the method" (Pestalozzi, 1809/1964d, p. 280). In his own enthusiasm for his concern (the implementation of the method), and also in his skepticism regarding whether the examiners could completely grasp the method, Pestalozzi offered the commission that would be sent by the Swiss confederate government "support" in the form of two documents enclosed with his letter. The first contained 37 questions concerning the method and the institute, and the second was a list of possible experts to conduct the evaluation—all of them Pestalozzians in the broadest sense (p. 285ff.).

The three commissioners chosen by the Legislative Assembly were not on Pestalozzi's list, but they can certainly be called Pestalozzi sympathizers. They were mandated to submit a comprehensive report describing the institute, explaining the benefits of the method, and assessing the "value" and practicability of the institute. Their report, *Bericht über die Pestalozzische Erziehungs-Anstalt zu Yverdon an Seine Excellenz den Herrn Landammann und die Hohe Tagsatzung der Schweizerischen Eydgenossenschaft* [Report on Pestalozzi's Education Institute at Yverdon for His Excellency Chief Magistrate and the Swiss Confederate Legislative Assembly] (Girard et al., 1810), over 200 pages long, was written based on a five-day visit to Yverdon. It was objective in tone and not without goodwill for Pestalozzi. But right at the beginning of the report, the commissioners stressed the "insular" character of the institute. Its members had developed "a language of their own" that in part closed themselves to outsiders.

Upon this background, the state commissioners recognized the uniqueness of the institute but rated it as an inimitable example. The report concluded, therefore, that Pestalozzi's institute could not act as a model for the public schools, because

- It was an institute that had a family character
- It offered its (rather wealthy) clientele corresponding instruction (which in this way could hardly be realized at normal schools)
- It had a not altogether convincing curriculum
- Its assertion that there was a connection between the school subjects and "the method" was not immediately clear or comprehensible.

Although the report contained diverse small tokens of praise, Pestalozzi's idea of applying his method to the public school system in Switzerland (and later Europe) with state support was rejected by the report:

> The institute is not set up at all in harmony with our public schools... The institute goes its own way, the public schools follow theirs, and it is not at all probable that they will ever meet. (Girard, 1810, p. 215)

Many other reports had attested to the effectiveness of the instruction at the institute. But the fact that the children learned, that they were also "motivated," was probably not an indication that the method was compelling and was probably due more to a conglomeration of historical circumstances that formed the framework conditions of the institute and made the type of institute that it was at all possible. Important were mainly mental factors that improved the motivation of the teachers. Pestalozzi's charisma and his rhetoric were strengthened by the fact that an educationalizing Europe had begun to see improved education as a way to prevent war and that the nations wanted to stabilize themselves and their futures via new school systems. There was also the circumstance that the public attention created by the media (newspapers, journals, books, travelogues, assessment reports) encouraged the teachers to teach better than would be expected under "normal" circumstances without this public attention. Most of the teachers taught about 50 lessons per week, and, what is more, they had constant duties caring for the children; they even had to sleep in the children's dormitories at night to supervise them. It is no wonder that in connection with various fierce arguments after 1810—that is, after the inspection report was made public—teacher overload became apparent, and it did further damage to the culture of the institute. After the public failure of the institute the disputes could no longer be held at bay by Pestalozzi's charisma. To the detriment of the institute the conflicts were now waged in public, which heralded a process of disintegration. The numbers documenting the actual collapse are impressive: in 1809, when Pestalozzi had requested the state evaluation, there were 165 pupils and 63 teachers and trainees at the institute, but in 1811, one year after publication of the report, there were 83 pupils and 41 teachers and trainees. In the free market of the school providers of the time, consumers had acted quickly.

However, even if the number of children at the institute of Yverdon never again reached the number of the top year in 1809, the decline was not final. Moreover, Pestalozzi remained the integrative figure of the educational transformation of the time. When, for instance, the Prussians were victorious against Napoleon's army in the context of the German campaign (Napoleonic Wars) in 1813, they—often copying the ideas of Fichte—designed the future of Germany. One of the prime examples is a publication by the German Lutheran theologian Friedrich Kohlrausch (1780–1867),[2] who gave public lectures on *Deutschlands Zukunft* [The Future of Germany] (Kohlrausch, 1814) in the autumn of 1813. In these lectures Kohlrausch (1814) discussed questions of the German unity, the coming of a new global era introduced by the Germans, the meaning of national symbols and national festivals, the importance of arts and mothers, and the crucial role of education in implementing this program. Having visited Pestalozzi—like countless others before and after him—in 1808, he sent his book to Pestalozzi with gratefulness for Pestalozzi's contribution to the benefit of the human race to which he, Kohlrausch, meant to contribute, too (Kohlrausch 1814/2012, p. 52). Building the future and education were indissolubly linked to each other, and Pestalozzi was the unsurpassable moral instance of this connection that remained unaffected by the turmoil in his institute.

10.2 Troubled years at the institute in Yverdon

The publication of the state commission's report was only a trigger and not the reason for the internal tensions at the institute. Before the report, the indisputable success and Pestalozzi's authority were able to cover up personal differences and organizational deficiencies, but now they suddenly became very evident. The crisis that ensued can be illustrated by two of Pestalozzi's staff members, who could not be more different and who both courted the favor of their master. They each formed different alliances to exert more influence on the weak management of the institute. One was Niederer, mentioned in Chapter 7, who had already joined Pestalozzi in Burgdorf in 1803 and who aimed to underpin the Pestalozzi method by the philosophy of German idealism. The other was Joseph Schmid (1785–1851) of Voralberg in Austria, who entered Burgdorf in 1801 as a pupil and had an impressive interinstitutional career that above and beyond his role as mathematics teacher would in the end make him Pestalozzi's most important member of staff.

The tensions between the two experts Niederer and Schmid were also personal, of course, but the conflict was only able to escalate because development of "the method" remained below public expectations and because the institute had not developed an efficient form of organization. Niederer and Schmid both felt called upon to solve the problems. Niederer tried to convince the public through his development of a "philosophy of the method"; however, this did not contribute anything to the development of instruction. Together with Pestalozzi he edited the *Wochenschrift für Menschenbildung* from 1807 to 1811 (in which also the Stans letter (Pestalozzi, 1807/1932) was printed for the first time). Niederer was the central editor, and he did not shy away from adding his own commentaries to Pestalozzi's texts. It was also Niederer who became involved in the public polemics triggered by the state evaluation report on the Yverdon institute and who, in 1811, published the exceptionally sharp-edged text, *Das Pestalozzische Institut an das Publikum. eine Schutzrede gegen verläumderische Angriffe* [The Pestalozzi Institute to the Public: A Defense to Defamatory Attacks] (Niederer, 1811). It was his attempt to defend Pestalozzi, the institute, and himself, and it only served to add more fuel to the fire.

At this point in time, Niederer's adversary Schmid was no longer in Yverdon. Previously, he had, without any mandate, taken on an organizational leadership role among the teaching staff, which the institute needed but not all of the staff members appreciated. Schmid had advised against having the state commission evaluate the institute, because he had recognized the great gulf between the public propaganda and the education reality. His realistic assessment, his lack of charisma, and his apparently standoffish and overbearing manner also did not endear him to many at the institute. Schmid resigned his post and left Yverdon in May 1810 to become head of the school in Bregenz, Austria. Shortly beforehand he had published a three-volume mathematics textbook (Schmid, 1809/1811) that paid homage to Pestalozzi; its success further publicized the name of the institute, and at the concrete level of instruction. It was titled *Die Elemente der Form und Grösse (gewöhnlich Geometrie genannt), nach Pestalozzis Grundsätzen bearbeitet* [The Elements of Form and Size (Usually Called Geometry), Handled According to Pestalozzi's Principles].

But the years without Schmid would make it clear that the institute needed firmer organization and in particular better management of finances. After long discussions, Schmid returned to Yverdon in 1815, the year when the death of Pestalozzi's wife Anna took a terrible toll on Pestalozzi's optimism. Schmid managed to improve the organization of the institute. But his return had reinforced him in his imperious manner, so much so that he was likened to a military officer. Krüsi, one of Pestalozzi's most important assistants—who had fled the chaos of war with children from eastern Switzerland in 1800 and moved to Burgdorf and worked with Pestalozzi ever since—had threatened to leave the institute already in 1808. But now Krüsi resigned and left, along with 15 other teachers, to start his own school in Yverdon. On Pentecost (Whit Sunday) in 1817 the high point of the disputes occurred: Niederer used his sermon in the church at Yverdon to break with Pestalozzi and his institute publicly. But instead of leaving Yverdon, Niederer moved to the girls' institute located right next to the institute. Pestalozzi had set it up shortly after arriving in Yverdon and had given it to Rosette Kasthofer (1779–1857), a successful teacher, in 1813. Niederer had married Kasthofer in 1814. From this point on, three schools existed within the very small area of Yverdon, which did not help to defuse the conflicts. Law suits and public battles were waged, with the result that in 1824 (when Pestalozzi was 78 years old), Schmid was expelled from the Canton of Vaud. This would turn out to be the death blow to the ailing institute.

10.3 *An die Unschuld, den Ernst und den Edelmut* (1815)

The internal problems at the institute were not the only difficulties that Pestalozzi had to face. The tensions across Europe with the military defeats of Napoleon and the Congress of Vienna (1814–1815) would turn out to be much more fruitful for his work. Europe faced the question as to whether it should return to the old order or risk a change, and it deliberated on where national boundaries should be drawn. Switzerland, which was still divided into factions, was threatened with being divided into two: eastern Switzerland was to go to Austria and western Switzerland to France. This chaos reactivated Pestalozzi's political socialization from the days of his youth and led him to write a long commentary on the events, *An die Unschuld, den Ernst und den Edelmut meines Zeitalters und meines Vaterlandes. Ein Wort zur Zeit* [To the Innocence, Seriousness, and Magnanimity of My Time and Mt Fatherland: A Word to the Time] (Pestalozzi, 1815/1977), which was published in 1815.

This work would be Pestalozzi's last word on the role of education with regard to the reestablishment of the republic of virtue. Pestalozzi had written a foreword to the commentary as a "citizen of Zurich," but the foreword was not published with the text. It expressed his preference for fraternal and local community life and his preference for the republican form of government—at least for Switzerland. Pestalozzi repeated in the foreword that the current problems, which he called "weakness of the world and the states," were the result of long historical processes and were not caused by the French Revolution. Rather, the problems had to be traced back to earlier offenses: "The Revolution is in its essence only a continuation of this weakness, but of course a continuation that degenerated and ran wild" (Pestalozzi, 1815/1977, p. 3).

Following that opening, Pestalozzi came to speak of the main purpose of politics, which for the now 68-year-old was practically the same as his ideals at age 34, as if there had been no American, French, or Helvetic Revolutions in the meantime. It was still his belief that government must mainly protect the individual households, whereby this ideal was in principle feasible also in monarchies and not only in monarchies. As an example Pestalozzi offered Austrian Empress Maria Theresa,[3] mother of Emperor Joseph II,[4] whom Pestalozzi had admired in the 1780s. Maria Theresa had demonstrated in Hungary how a nation in the greatest crisis could be united and in doing so had created a political reality that was not inferior to the political reality of well-organized republics. Whatever worked in monarchies, Pestalozzi wrote, must fit even better in republics. The point was to overcome the social segregation of "upper" and "lower," and the means to do so was education that was in accordance with human nature: "My politics begin and end with education" (Pestalozzi, 1815/1977, p. 12).

In this connection Pestalozzi declared himself a republican in the sense of the (Swiss) republic of virtue:

> And I say even more so—I am a republican but not a republican for big nations. I am a republican for small but magnanimous republican-organized city and country communities; and of these I say: The sanctuary of the sovereign power can in these communities rise to heights whose psychological beneficial effect on the refinement of the individuals is not achievable in the widespread size of a monarchy. (Pestalozzi, 1815/1977, p. 10)

The key to a noble republic of virtue was politics, on the one hand, which as *conditio sine qua non* had to create legal relationships that in turn made it possible for people to have secure economic livelihoods and not to develop all too great social disparities among them. Economically well-provided for by working fathers, mothers and their children could form a relationship of trust in the home. In that trusting relationship, children would develop naturally and mature into religiously shaped virtuousness. And as if—five years after the state commissioners' evaluation report on the institute (Girard, 1810)—Pestalozzi wanted to once again defend the public relevance of his educational concept, he criticized the public school system and propagated his "education in closeness": "Our race educates itself fundamentally only face to face, and heart to heart humanly" (Pestalozzi, 1815/1977, p. 19).

This related popular education to national unity and traced the political future back to education, which on its part was based on religion and thus became the most important human practice: "Human education is God's way and nature's way and thus the highest art of our race; man must seek it and value it as his highest good" (Pestalozzi, 1815/1977, p. 23). With this, Pestalozzi was right in line with the mood in Europe, which—after Napoleon had once again kept Europe in suspense for 100 days[5]—wanted only one thing: to go back to the old conditions ("Restoration") and to have lasting peace. In Europe's view, popular education, at first very limited and fostering religion and obedience, would guarantee that peace. Despite the weighty problems in his institute and the decreased demand for places at the institute, Pestalozzi remained for some years the cult figure in this educationalized world of the Restoration.

10.4   The new school for the poor

After many long-serving staff members and teachers left after 1815, Schmid was the mainstay of the institute in Yverdon. To solve the financial crisis he managed to negotiate a contract with Cotta, the famous publishing house in Stuttgart, which advanced Pestalozzi the considerable sum of 50,000 francs for publication of his collected works. Cotta's edition of Pestalozzi's complete works was published in 15 volumes from 1819 to 1826. The subscriptions to this edition show how large Pestalozzi's network in Europe had become: from April 1817 to January 1818, the total number of subscriptions had reached 1,850. This success is all the more astounding, as 1816 was the "Year Without a Summer"[6] in Europe, due among other things to the effects on the weather of the eruption of Mount Tambora on the island of Sumbawa, Indonesia, in 1815. It led to failed harvests and major food shortages; the price of foodstuffs rose sharply. What is more, the effects of the Napoleonic Wars and the lifting of the Continental System were not at all overcome. The result was a profound economic crisis. Considering the price of the edition, the number of subscribers to Pestalozzi's collected works seems therefore very high: a single volume was to cost 2.5 Swiss francs, 1 guilders 45 *Kreutzer* (silver coin and unit of currency in the southern German states), or 1 Saxon *Thaler*; the planned 12 volumes of the collected works would cost 30 francs.[7]

A recent study that examined the list of subscribers (Caluori, Horlacher, and Tröhler, 2012) demonstrated impressively the composition of Europe's new educational public, which had national emphases for language reasons alone.[8] Among the few women subscribers, representatives of the aristocracy dominated, but among the 1,224 men that subscribed, only 91 persons (less than 10%) came from the nobility: the educational public was an (upper) middle-class public. The largest occupational group among the subscribers, with 227 persons, worked in education as teachers, heads of institutes, or educators. The second largest occupational group, almost as large with 221 persons, worked in government as public officials. Pastors made up another large occupational group among the subscribers, with pastors often working also as teachers. Subscribers representing the free professions worked in banking, manufacturing, business, and trade (107 persons), as jurists and notaries (22 persons), and as doctors and pharmacists (38 persons). Finally, 19 subscribers worked in the military.

However, Pestalozzi did not use the money brought in by this success only for improvement of the institute. Instead, and much to Schmid's dismay, he used it to found a home for poor children, a project that Pestalozzi had not worked on much in the preceding ten years. Educating the poor to secure their livelihood was and remained the republican main duty of the privileged, because only on this basis via education could virtue be transmitted. In September 1818, Pestalozzi—now 72 years old—opened a facility in Clindy, just a few minutes away on foot from the Yverdon institute, for 12 children that were either orphans or had been abandoned by their families. As if he had a guilty conscience for not having worked with educating the poor for so long, Pestalozzi was committed to this smaller-scale endeavor, and the organizational demands were much better suited to him personally than those of the large institute. After only a few months, enrollment at the home had grown to nearly 30 children. Under Schmid's influence, the home in Clindy did not develop into an industry school with training in skilled trades and proto-industries but instead became a place to train teachers for country schools. The young (poor) people were to be trained as country schoolteachers who would themselves educate and cultivate the poor. With this, the educationalization of coping with social injustices in the corrupt republic had reached a high point, which pleased Pestalozzi. As he wrote to his friend Nicolovius in Berlin in 1819: "My work is saved. God saved my work. It flourishes in my home for the poor with strength and surety that make every hour of my current life the brightest blessing" (Pestalozzi, 1819/1969, p. 311). He praised the selfless commitment on the part of Schmid and Schmid's sister Katharina Schmid (1799–1853), who would marry Pestalozzi's nephew, Gottlieb Pestalozzi (1797–1863) in 1822. And he reported: "I am happy. As unhappy as I was before, so happy am I now" (p. 311).

The financial problems continued, however. Schmid persuaded Pestalozzi to move the home for the poor in Clindy into the institute in Yverdon, but this had consequences. Although after 1810 and also after 1817 the institute had had fewer enrollments than in 1808–1809, interest mainly on the part of private parties did not let up. With the end of the Continental System in 1814, the English traveled on the continent more and more, which suddenly made closer contacts with England possible. The interest of many Englishmen in "the Pestalozzi method" led to an "English colony" in Yverdon for which even their own hotel was built. The English eased the institute's financial burden, but when the poor children were moved from Clindy to the Yverdon castle, the result was a kind of two-tier society. The English children came from the better classes and paid for their training, whereas the children from Clindy were not charged tuition, of course. To set the rich children at ease, Pestalozzi's solution was to have the poor children work for their stay and in part to serve the children from wealthy families. This only worsened the tensions. The children from poor families that had to serve the residents from rich families did not understand why they should have this subordinate role in the context of life at the institute.

It would turn out that the great political-social vision of a republic with relatively small social disparities and citizens interacting in fraternal friendship under one roof would be difficult to manage even in Yverdon. The differing educational needs of children from different social classes and the children's social difficulties living together in the institute—the children of poorer families had to work to come up for the costs by helping to serve the children of the richer families—contributed to the further decline of an institute whose reputation was already tarnished by the publicly conducted conflicts between former staff members and Pestalozzi and by a lengthy court battle between the institute and Niederer's institute for girls. It did not ease the situation that the head of the institute, who was now over 75 years old, became more inflexible and had blind faith in Schmid. Even though Pestalozzi won the court battle, when the English left Yverdon in 1822–1823, the institute was on the verge of collapse.

Notes

1. http://en.wikipedia.org/wiki/Philipp_Emanuel_von_Fellenberg
2. http://en.wikipedia.org/wiki/Heinrich_Friedrich_Theodor_Kohlrausch
3. http://en.wikipedia.org/wiki/Maria_Theresa
4. http://en.wikipedia.org/wiki/Joseph_II,_Holy_Roman_Emperor
5. http://en.wikipedia.org/wiki/Hundred_Days
6. http://en.wikipedia.org/wiki/Year_Without_a_Summer
7. For comparison: the (day) wage for a man in the textile industry was 7 Swiss centimes and for a woman 5 centimes. In other words, textile workers would have had to work almost one and a half years to earn 30 francs. A 2.2-pound loaf of bread cost 43 centimes in 1820, 2.2 pounds of potatoes 4 centimes, 2.2 pounds of beef 64 centimes. One school year at the institute in Yverdon (in 1814) was considerably more costly—namely, 300 francs (and in 1817, 30 new *Louis d'or*); this was the basic fee, not including fees for laundry, excursions, or school materials.
8. Most of the subscriptions came from Germany (a total of 756); Switzerland was in second place, with 324 subscriptions. Two other countries with a high number of subscribers were Poland and Hungary, with 68 subscriptions each. In Poland, 50 of the subscribers were in Silesia; in Hungary, a similarly large number of the subscribers were in Budapest. In Austria, where 51 persons subscribed, with the greatest number of subscribers were in Vienna (24) and in Vorarlberg (20). In France most of the subscribers (33 out of the total of 37) were in Alsace. In Italy, all 12 subscribers were in Northern Italy. Considering country size, The Netherlands heads the top of the list, with 19 subscribers. In Latvia (13 subscriptions) and Estonia (14), most of the subscribers were in the cities Riga and Tallinn. In Russia (22 subscriptions), 8 subscribers were in St Petersburg and 7 in Königsberg. Pestalozzi's network does not appear to have been strong in the Scandinavian countries: the subscribers in Denmark and in Norway appear to be single cases. And based on the number of subscribers, Pestalozzi's network was also weak in the English-speaking countries: there were 3 subscribers in Ireland, 1 subscriber in Scotland, and 3 subscribers in the United States.

11
The Educationalized World and the Internationalization of the Cult of Pestalozzi

Abstract: *Despite some serious interest on the part of English philanthropists around 1820, the decline of Yverdon was inexorable, especially when former collaborators started a public campaign against their now 75-year-old hero. Pestalozzi moved back to his Neuhof estate, determined to found a new educational institution for the poor. Public attacks shattered his health; he died in 1827 at the age of 81. After his death, there were numerous aspirants to Pestalozzi's intellectual inheritance, even among his enemies. In 1830, the July Revolution in France resulted in a constitutional monarchy. This initiated the Europe-wide process of the end of the Restoration and a year of revolution in Europe. The territorial states, as they had been defined at the Congress of Vienna in 1815, used their new constitutions to legitimatize themselves as nation-states, while also officially declaring their need for modern mass schooling. Pestalozzi became the hero among the main actors of this institutionalization of teaching*

Tröhler, Daniel. *Pestalozzi and the Educationalization of the World.* New York: Palgrave Macmillan, 2013.
DOI: 10.1057/9781137346858.

11.1 The final collapse of the institute in Yverdon

With the defeat of Napoleon and the Congress of Vienna, Europe saw the dawning of a new age, which Swiss jurist Karl Ludwig von Haller (1768–1854), a prominent opponent of Pestalozzi, called "Restoration." This Restoration took on more and more conservative and rigid forms after 1820, and Pestalozzi's republican vision of the economically secure family as a haven of education in virtue was rather alien to the spirit of the times. There was practically no more demand on the part of other countries for Pestalozzi's education. The steadily decreasing success put massive pressure on the institute, which—with an aged Pestalozzi effectively no longer able to lead and with an ever more domineering Schmid—was in a state of permanent conflict. All attempts by sympathizers to remove Schmid from the teaching staff failed because of a veto by Pestalozzi, who was perceived to be in a relation of mental bondage to Schmid. The well-meant advice of his friends put additional pressure on Pestalozzi, and he withdrew considerably from the outside world and developed a stubbornly defiant attitude towards anything that seemed to call him or Schmid into question.

Reports by the few remaining *Eleven* were full of skepticism and led—in the case of Prussia—to a final dwindling down of the exchange, even though Nicolovius, who had been a close friend of Pestalozzi, was now head of the culture and education section at the Prussian ministry of the interior. Alongside the internal tensions, the financial difficulties that followed when the Prussian teacher trainees and the English colony left Yverdon in 1822 were yet another problem that Pestalozzi was facing. In addition, he had quarreled with the cantonal authorities, whom he reproached for failing to support his own institute and for unfairly supporting the other institutes in Yverdon—Niederer's institute and Krüsi's institute—that had after all grown out of his. The authorities at first acted as moderators and did not do what Pestalozzi had hoped—namely, officially close the other two institutes. Tensions increased, and Jeremias Meyer (1798–1852), a former student at the institute, added fuel to the fire with his publications *Wie Herr Joseph Schmid die Pestalozzische Anstalt leitet* [How Mr. Joseph Schmid Leads the Pestalozzi Institute] (Meyer, 1822) and *Aux amis de Pestalozzi* [To the Friends of Pestalozzi] (Meyer, 1823). The latter work was a response to Schmid's *Wahrheit und Irrtum in Pestalozzis Lebensschicksalen* [Truth and Error in Pestalozzi's Life Destinies] (Schmid, 1822), which was also very contentious.

These (and other) publications garnered a great deal of attention, which shows how very strong the interest in Pestalozzi was in Europe. However, these publications forced the state council, the executive body of the canton, to act. Schmid was recognized as being the main cause of the arguments in Yverdon and was expelled from the Canton of Vaud on October 6, 1824. Pestalozzi's protest and his request to the state council to have Schmid brought back were based on the argument that he suspected intrigue and conspiracy; Pestalozzi also threatened to leave the canton with Schmid, if Schmid were required to go: "*Je quitte le canton avec lui*" [I will leave the canton with him] (Pestalozzi, 1824/1971a, p. 183). Pestalozzi repeated his views in a letter to the city council of Yverdon, in which he also reminded that he had never sought asylum in Yverdon and therefore was not a supplicant; on the contrary, it had been the city council that had asked Pestalozzi to settle in Yverdon, tempting him with the promise of all possible support (Pestalozzi, 1824/1971b, p. 188). In another letter a few days later Pestalozzi reminded the city council of his great service to the city and began to threaten that he would seek recompense for all financial expenses incurred in Yverdon (Pestalozzi, 1824/1971c, p. 189f.). When Pestalozzi indeed left Yverdon at the start of 1825, heading for Neuhof, which still belonged to him, he believed that the Yverdon castle was still in his possession and that a successor there could further develop "the method." However, the municipality let him know that he was no longer entitled to use the castle once he left Yverdon.

At Neuhof Pestalozzi found a "new" family that strengthened his tie with Schmid even more: living there were Schmid's sister Katharina and Pestalozzi's grandson Gottlieb, who had married in 1822. Their son Heinrich Karl Pestalozzi (1825–1891) was Pestalozzi's only great-grandchild. At the end of 1825 and the start of 1826 Pestalozzi tried with his grandson to become reestablished in the castle in Yverdon, but the attempts failed and he resigned himself to having to stay at Neuhof. At least on January 12, 1826, on the occasion of his 80th birthday, he received some honors that bolstered his visibly weakened self-esteem. However, that did not stop him from publishing the obstinate book, *Meine Lebensschicksale als Vorsteher meiner Erziehungsinstitute in Burgdorf und Iferten* [My Life's Destiny as Head of my Education Institutes in Burgdorf and Iferten] (Pestalozzi, 1826a), in which he, in a peculiar way, presents himself as a clumsy simpleton who had gained true strength only with Schmid. This surprising turn gave Pestalozzi the foundation upon which in defending Schmid he could take a swing against everyone that he saw as his enemies. But the book did not trigger outraged responses; rather, it was viewed as an embarrassment, and it sealed the already held judgment that Pestalozzi—now 80 years old—was no longer really of sound mind. However, there would be one exception to this noble silence: a public reply statement in January 1827 that was very painful for Pestalozzi.

11.2 The last new beginning and the end at Neuhof

At this time, Schmid was in France and in England to scout out new terrain for his master. In addition to *Meine Lebensschicksale* Pestalozzi published a second book (Pestalozzi, 1826b) that contained no polemics and explained the basis of "the Pestalozzi method" again and in a remarkably clear manner. The title of the publication, *Schwanengesang* [Swan Song] seems to hint at Pestalozzi's approaching death,[1] and once again he linked his theoretical explanations on the method with a broad biographical excursus: his life bore witness to the infallibility of the method. Besides this last epic, Pestalozzi worked on further development of the method, in particular on simplifying language acquisition, and he tried to revive his network through extensive correspondence: after *Meine Lebensschicksale* and *Schwanengesang* were published, Pestalozzi wrote over 70 letters to people all over the world.

Development and dissemination of "the method" was only one of Pestalozzi's aims, however; the other was his concern for the disadvantaged. In mid-1825—50 years after his first attempt at Neuhof—he drew up a new plan for an industrial school at Neuhof. As he told Schmid in a letter (Pestalozzi, 1825/1971d), it would (again) bring together agriculture, industry, and education, although he was aware that this had led to failure in his youthful years (p. 273, p. 275). To this purpose, Pestalozzi began to build a house next to his manor for the poor children that he planned to take in. However, the plan never became reality. He was also pursuing a plan to support a people's bookstore or a people's publishing house—advised by "experts on the people" and "cleansed of all corruption of people's interest in reading [meaning useless, amusing works]"—and an art collection that would transmit to the people elementary and necessary insights and would lead to a true people's culture and the people's true humanization (p. 276). Big plans—but none of them came to fruition.

Pestalozzi was in good health in 1826, so that he could hope to make Neuhof a center of educational resurrection of the people. However, a book about him published in 1827 was a terrible blow. It was written by 25-year-old Eduard Biber (1801–1874) of Württemberg, Germany, who had worked as a teacher at Niederer's institute in Yverdon from 1823 to 1825. The book, *Beitrag zur Biographie Pestalozzi's* [Contributions to Pestalozzi's Biography] (Biber, 1827), was over 300 pages long and probably came out at the end of 1826. It was a response to Pestalozzi's (1826) *Mein Lebensschicksale*. Biber had all too apparently become a mouthpiece for Niederer, against whom Pestalozzi had made serious accusations in *Meine Lebensschicksale*. Biber had access to all private and court documents and fought as an advocate for Niederer after the event, so to speak. Biber presented Pestalozzi's turning from Niederer to Schmid as a betrayal caused by Pestalozzi's weakness and Schmid's malice. But in contrast to other polemics, Biber aimed his criticisms directly at Pestalozzi himself as a person, towards the end of the book accusing Pestalozzi of an entire catalogue of misdemeanors and errors and even of slander (Biber, 1827, pp. 315–320).[2] Pestalozzi's strategy of supporting the dignity of "the method" autobiographically through his own life was doomed to fail if his life was told as a history of slanders rather than of moral purity.

Pestalozzi's immediate response to Biber's book was outrage; he was appalled and hurt. Existing handwritten notes show that he must have been very much distraught and ill as he tried to write a reply, since for pages at a time, he forgot to dip his feather nib into the ink, and whole passages have to be read as "etchings" without ink. His reaction is characteristic, for he once again focused on his suffering: "Oh, my sufferings are inexpressible," begin Pestalozzi's first lines written at the end of January 1827, which were meant to show the world's ungrateful attitude towards his work:

> People despise me as a feeble, infirm old man; they no longer think me good for anything; I do but excite their derision. It is not, however, for myself that I am troubled, but for my idea, which shares my fate. My most sacred possession, the belief that has inspired the whole of my long and painful life, is scornfully trodden under foot. To die is nothing; I even welcome death, for I am weary and would fain be at rest; but to have lived a life of sacrifice and to have failed, to see my work destroyed and go down with it to the grave, this is frightful, more frightful than I can express. Would that I could weep, but my tears refuse to flow. And you, my poor ones, the oppressed,

despised and rejected of this world; you too, alas! Will be forsaken and ridiculed, even as I am. (Pestalozzi, 1827/1976a, p. 351; English translation from de Guimps, 2004/1890, p. 364)

Pestalozzi did not live to see that a reply on his part, which he was unable to complete, would not have been necessary, as reception of Biber's book was almost unanimously negative (Morf, 1889, p. 554ff; Dejung, 1976, p. 482ff.), so that in the end, it was Schmid who emerged from the whole affair with a stronger image in the public opinion. Even old critics of Pestalozzi rejected the aggressive pasquil, and Niederer spent a lot of time trying to calm the waters. Niederer's wife, Rosette Niederer Kasthofer, whom Pestalozzi had appointed head of the institute for girls in Yverdon, wrote Pestalozzi a letter (Kasthofer, 1827/in press), in the wake of the outrage, accusing him in an extremely hateful way of bearing the blame for everything. Obviously filled with hate as well as short-lived satisfaction with Biber's book, Kasthofer (1827/in press) wrote:

> I wish to speak to you once more before Death takes hold of you. The present must be terrible for you, for the truth is revealed between us and you. Biber's book is perhaps in your hands now. It is dreadful for you, because it is true. Oh, may it chasten you! (freely translated here)

Crowing with a religious metaphor, she continued: "Poor man, what Hell must you be experiencing as your faults are uncovered" (Kasthofer, 1827/in press). However, Kasthofer's letter never reached Pestalozzi, as it was sent from Yverdon on the day that Pestalozzi died.

At the end of January 1827, Pestalozzi's health had greatly deteriorated. On February 13 his doctor diagnosed various afflictions and general weakness but also infection of the eyes, lack of sleep, weak bladder muscles, and constipation—which were all said to be due to Pestalozzi's unceasing work on his reply to Biber's attack. His condition became so grave that on February 15, his grandson Gottlieb and his grandson's wife Katharina took him by sled to Brugg to be closer to medical help, even though Pestalozzi seemed to be in good cheer about prospects of returning home to Neuhof. However, two days later, on the morning of February 17, 1827, he died a calm and peaceful death according to the medical report. He was buried with a ceremony next to the old schoolhouse in Birr on February 19. Some prominent personages attended the burial, but it was hardly commensurate with Pestalozzi's international fame. Pestalozzi had written his own epitaph for his gravestone; it was not without bitterness, and in the end it was not used: "On his grave a rose will blossom, the sight of which will makes those eyes cry that stayed dry in the face of his suffering" (Pestalozzi, 1976b/1827, p. 380; freely translated here).

11.3 Death and the start of a cult

After Pestalozzi's death, there were numerous aspirants to Pestalozzi's intellectual inheritance. First and foremost was Schmid, whom Pestalozzi in his last will and testament of February 15, 1827 designated executor of his plans (Pestalozzi, 1976c/1827). But also Niederer was suddenly forgiving, in that he made a distinction between Pestalozzi the (mortal) man and Pestalozzi the spiritual man and in this way tried to put himself forward as Pestalozzi's rightful heir. In a column called *Pestalozziana* in the journal *Rheinisch-westfälische Monatschrift für Erziehung und Volksunterricht* [Rhenish-Westphalian Monthly Journal of Education and Public Instruction], Niederer, together with two other former members of Pestalozzi's staff, published *Erklärung zu Pestalozzis Tode* [Statement on Pestalozzi's Death], which they had written directly after Pestalozzi's death:

> Pestalozzi now once again becomes all that he was to us at the beginning. The grave forgives all. It forever covers all that of men that is mortal... Also we will continue the work—with God, courage, and humility, being unwaveringly loyal to the true Pestalozzi and forgetting all insult. (Niederer, Krüsi, and Näf, 1827, 70)

With Pestalozzi now deceased, the aim was to honor him but also, as Pestalozzi's heirs, to attain stronger influence in an educationalized world. The political events in Europe would further reinforce this educationalization.

In 1830, three years after Pestalozzi's death, the July Revolution in France saw the final overthrow of the Bourbon monarchy and once again seizure of power by the bourgeoisie, resulting in a constitutional monarchy and thus initiating the Europe-wide process of the end of the Restoration and a year of revolution in Europe.[3] The territorial states as they had been defined at the Congress of Vienna in 1815 began to give themselves a legitimate basis as nation-states and—with the exception of reactionary Prussia and England—gave themselves constitutions. They included the Kingdoms of Saxon, Kingdom of Hanover, Hessen-Kassel, Duchy of Braunschweig, and then Belgium, Luxembourg, and the cantons of Switzerland, led by Zurich, which had a new, liberal constitution already in 1831. A remarkable thing about this political reorientation was that everywhere where new constitutions were passed, new school laws were issued almost immediately. For the first time in history, these school laws laid down comprehensive public school attendance. France passed the Charter of 1830[4] as well as the Guizot[5] school law establishing primary education for all citizens in 1833. Belgium established a constitution in 1831 and a comprehensive school law in 1842. This delay was due to the fact that in 1830 Belgium together with Luxembourg separated from The Netherlands, which led to a lengthy dispute that ended only in 1839 with the independence of today's Luxembourg—separate from Belgium. Luxembourg enacted its own constitution in 1841 and a school law in 1843. Events in Switzerland were similar: the Canton of Zurich passed a constitution in 1831 and a comprehensive school law in 1832, and the Canton of Bern had a new constitution in 1832 and a new school law in 1833. The nation-states, legitimized by their constitutions, evidently banked on the importance of the school for their existence. Nation building was an educational program and the nation-states were the heirs and catalysts of the educational turn. They invested a lot of money in this development, drove the church out of its position of supremacy, established compulsory schooling, began to develop curricula, and—above all—systematically organized teacher education. Moreover, they all looked with interest and even jealousy at what the other nations were doing in the area of the school system and strove to implement successful models of other countries in their own.

In the redesign of the school system that had become possible with these political changes, the Pestalozzians played a role to some extent, but the concept of "the Pestalozzi method," which in the end targeted education at home and thus mothers, did not really fit the modern school system. This criticism had already been raised in 1810 in the state commissioners' evaluation report on the Pestalozzi institute in Yverdon (Girard et al., 1810) and was not any less true now. Nevertheless, Pestalozzi was not forgotten, especially not in Germany, and by a very specific group. Teachers, who were becoming more and more self-aware, had found in Pestalozzi their "patron saint," a figurehead that was wonderfully suited for pushing through their professional interests. One of the central coordinators of this Pestalozzi Renaissance was Adolph Diesterweg

(1790–1866),[6] who in 1828–1829 had argued with Niederer about just how practicable the method really was.[7] For teachers, especially teachers in Prussia, Pestalozzi did not serve as a guide to instruction but rather as the idol of their profession.

To this purpose, events in honor of Pestalozzi's 100th birthday would be useful for this purpose. To honor Pestalozzi on his 99th birthday and celebrate his 100th year of life, Diesterweg and two other Pestalozzians published *Die Feier des 100sten Geburtstages Heinrich Pestalozzi's in Berlin am 12. Januar 1845: Vorfeier des hundertjährigen Jubiläums seiner Geburt am 12. Januar 1846* [Celebration of Heinrich Pestalozzi's Birthday in Berlin on 12 January 1845: An Early Celebration of the 100th Anniversary of His Birth on 12 January 1845] (Diesterweg, Kalisch, and Massmann, 1845). Also in 1845, Diesterweg published a literary hymn to Pestalozzi titled *Heinrich Pestalozzi: ein Wort über ihn und seine unsterblichen Verdienste, für die Kinder und deren Eltern, zu dem ersten Säcularfeste seiner Geburt* [Heinrich Pestalozzi: A Word on Him and His Important Merits, For the Children and Their Parents, on the Occasion of the First Commemoration of the Anniversary of His Birth] (Diesterweg, 1845), and on January 12, 1846 it was Diesterweg who gave the important speech at the celebration in honor of Pestalozzi in Berlin (Diesterweg, 1846).

These events made 1846 a year of an unparalleled Pestalozzi cult, which hardly anyone could ignore. In Germany, contrary to the facts, Pestalozzi was held to be the founder of the modern public school, thus raising its value, from which the teachers wanted to profit. Germany, and especially Prussia, would play a decisive role in the further dissemination of the educational turn. Although in Prussia a comprehensive schooling law drafted in 1819 had been rejected due to reactionary power politics, efforts to educate able subjects were carried on unbroken. Organized teacher education was a part of this, and it was developed very early: as early as in 1825 there were 28 teacher education seminaries in Prussia, and 12 years later in 1837 there were 45 (Sauer, 1987, p. 20f.). This organized form of teacher education attracted international interest. In the course of the reorganization of the school system in France, the French philosopher and cultural theorist Victor Cousin[8] traveled to Germany. Impressed by what he observed, Cousin published a report, *Rapport sur l'état de l'instruction publique dans quelques pays de l'Allemagne, et particulièrement en Prusse* (Cousin, 1832), that was published in English translation in the United States as early as 1835 (*Report on the State of Public Instruction in Prussia; Addressed to the Count de Montalivet. With Plans of*

School Houses) (Cousin, 1835) and caused a sensation. As a result of this, in 1843 Horace Mann (1796–1859),[9] who in 1837 was elected secretary of the newly formed Massachusetts Board of Education, traveled to Europe to visit schools, especially in Prussia. Mann published his observations in *Seventh Annual Report of the [Massachusetts] Board of Education, Together with the Seventh Annual Report of the Secretary of the Board* (Mann, 1844a).[10] His report became very well-known and was published in many editions. A few years later, Massachusetts adopted the Prussian education system and served as a model for reforms of other systems, mainly in the State of New York.

The Massachusetts Board of Education was the very first state board of education to be created in the United States. Other states followed over the next years, and they often looked to Europe: the educational turn had reached also the young republic prior to the mid-nineteenth century. The year 1826 had seen the publication of a first journal, the *American Journal of Education*; it was discontinued in 1830, however. A later journal of the same name fared better: it was published starting in 1856 by Henry Barnard[11] of Connecticut, who served as the first federal commissioner of education from 1867 to 1870 in the newly created federal Department of Education (which later became the Office of Education).[12] Even though in America the school was local, the importance assigned to education had inspired the creation of a national institution whose primary task was to report on the state of the schools in the country.

The *American Journal of Education* published by Barnard would be crucial for the transatlantic and transnational movement. One year before Mann's trip, Barnard himself was in Europe from 1835 to 1836 to learn about different forms of teacher education. He published his findings in 1851 in *Normal Schools and Other Institutions, Agencies, and Means Designed for Professional Education of Teachers* (Barnard, 1851). A few years later, after another stay in Europe, Barnard wrote a comprehensive work titled *National Education in Europe Being an Account of the Organization, Administration, Instruction, and Statistics of Public Schools of Different Grades in the Principle States* (Barnard, 1854), which mentioned almost all of the European states but focused mainly on Germany (64 pages), Prussia (173 pages), Switzerland (40 pages), France (104 pages), Ireland (44 pages), and England (169 pages). Two years later the first issue of the *American Journal of Education* was published. Almost all of the issues of the journal contained numerous contributions on Europe, and they were often translations. For instance, Pestalozzi was made known by a translation of a paper by Carl von Raumer, "The life and educational system of Pestalozzi" (Raumer, 1857), which in the same issue was followed directly by a paper by William F. Phelps (the first principal of the New Jersey State Normal School at Trenton, and the founder and president of the National Education Association), titled "Normal schools, their relations to primary and higher institutions of learning, and to the progress of society" (Phelps, 1857). Social progress and schooling were set in relation to the education of teachers, and Pestalozzi—even if he was not always mentioned explicitly—had become an indispensable element in this system of reasoning.

Notes

1 http://en.wikipedia.org/wiki/Swan_song
2 Biber emigrated to England in 1826. Older Pestalozzi research concludes that this book on Pestalozzi had ruined his chance of a career in continental Europe. Biber appears to have run a few schools in London, and after publishing a book called *Christian Education, in a Course of Lectures* (Biber, 1830), Biber—in a reversal of his 1826 book—began to transmit Pestalozzi to English readers with admiration: *Henry Pestalozzi and His Plan of Education: Being an Account of His Life and Writings with Copious Extracta from His Works and Extensive Details Illustrative of the Practical Parts of His Method* (Biber, 1831).
3 http://en.wikipedia.org/wiki/July_Revolution
4 http://en.wikipedia.org/wiki/Charter_of_1830
5 http://en.wikipedia.org/wiki/François_Guizot
6 http://en.wikipedia.org/wiki/Adolph_Diesterweg
7 Diesterweg wrote mockingly about how former enemies of Pestalozzi suddenly called themselves his heirs after his death (Diesterweg, 1828, p. 93). Niederer responded very aggressively by attacking Diesterweg sharply (Niederer, 1829), whereupon Diesterweg exposed Niederer publicly by noting that in school education real teaching problems had to be solved instead of getting carried away in philosophical speculations about the idea of teaching (Diesterweg, 1829).
8 http://en.wikipedia.org/wiki/Victor_Cousin
9 http://en.wikipedia.org/wiki/Horace_Mann
10 This report caused some teachers to protest: *Remarks on the Seventh Annual Report of the Hon. Horace Mann, Secretary of the Massachusetts Board of Education* (Association of Masters of the Boston Public Schools, 1844). Mann

responded in the same year in *Reply to the "Remarks" of Thirty-One Boston Schoolmasters on the Seventh Annual Report of the Secretary of the Massachusetts Board of Education* (Mann, 1844b), which in turn triggered further responses.

11 http://en.wikipedia.org/wiki/Henry_Barnard
12 http://en.wikipedia.org/wiki/Bureau_of_Education_(National)

12
Pestalozzi, or an Ambiguous Legacy in Education

Abstract: *The cultural shift of the educationalization of the world was not interrupted with the death of Pestalozzi but continued to grow in importance, not least because an increasingly self-confidant new profession—trained and certified teachers—were defending their interests by referring to the "educational saint" Pestalozzi. Teacher education, on the other hand, needed the teachers to identify with their national and moral duties, and with that, Pestalozzi became a hero of historiography, praised (wrongly) as the founder of the modern school and uniting the allegedly essential characteristics of a teacher: moral character and devotion. It was through this double interest—professional-political interest on the part of the teachers and national-moral interest on the part of the teacher educators—that Pestalozzi became the star of an educationalized culture that has expanded its cultural jurisdiction uninterruptedly to the present day.*

Tröhler, Daniel. *Pestalozzi and the Educationalization of the World*. New York: Palgrave Macmillan, 2013.
DOI: 10.1057/9781137346858.

12.1 Modernization and school

The period during which Pestalozzi died and the cult surrounding him became established is usually called the Restoration. This was also the epoch that began with the Congress of Vienna (1814–1815) and in which the political and social structures were to be restored that had been in place prior to the French Revolution and Napoleon. However, the program of the Restoration was not carried out very successfully in the long term—neither in the economy nor in national politics and definitely not in the area of education. Prussia, which the American school reformers took in part as a model, is an impressive example here. There was no industrial revolution in Prussia and no political revolution bringing increased participation for the citizens. And, as the only continental European country to do so, Prussia refused to have a constitution, which would have defined the legal relationships among the people. Comprehensive reform of national education, for which the reformers and Pestalozzi sympathizers—Georg Heinrich Ludwig Nicolovius, Johann Wilhelm Süvern, and Bernhard Christoph Ludwig Natorp—had paved the way, failed due to Prussia's increasingly reactionary politics.[1] Policies were not nationally oriented nor did they seek to educate the masses such that they would gain access to upper secondary education. An organized, structured school system bound to the principle of individual achievement (meritocracy) was introduced in Prussia only after the First World War.

It was Talcott Parsons, who—in the style of the modernization theories typical at the time—identified three revolutions as the essence of modernization: industrial, democratic, and educational, whereby the educational revolution would result from the first two (Parsons, 1971). Jeismann (1995) pointed out that in Prussia it was the other way around, that an educational revolution (despite the reactionary turn after 1819) took place without requiring the other two revolutions (industrial and democratic): "the educational revolution preceded the industrial and political" (p. 21). The educational revolution that Parsons and Jeismann spoke of can be seen as an expression of the educational turn—that is, the tendency to view social problems as educational challenges. It is no coincidence that after being defeated by Napoleon in 1806, Prussia responded with a revolution from above—with comprehensive education reform. Of this reform, however, in terms of institutions only today's Humboldt-Universität zu Berlin and the reorganization of the

Gymnasium (university preparatory upper secondary school) were realized, because they educated the state's future officials. Modern Prussia was an ultraconservative monarchy without a constitution that was backed by a privileged and loyal civil service, the members of which were educated at highly selective *Gymnasien*.

However, this situation did not prevent the numerous regional and local authorities from implementing school system reforms without uniform legal bases. And it was these reform activities, which varied greatly from region to region, that were observed by the visitors from other countries. These visits by interested persons from abroad were in line with the educational travels of the late eighteenth century, whereby the visits to Pestalozzi, as Jeismann (1995) rightly emphasized, marked the turning point from the older to the more modern travels: "With regard to both time and matter, the famous travels to Pestalozzi in Ifferten [Yverdon] mark the exact turning point that distinguishes the earlier and more personal of the eighteenth century, directed toward particular model schools, from the travels of the nineteenth century. The former still show a touch of the wish to hit upon curiosities; the latter were, above all, political expeditions with a public purpose" (p. 22).

Jeismann's (1995) analysis of the travel reports also showed, however, that the reporters did not deal with the educational policy tensions in Prussia (p. 27) and instead focused on classroom practices. Horace Mann praised the Prussian teachers, who "mingled with their pupils, passing rapidly from one side of the class to the other, animating, encouraging, sympathizing, breathing life into less active natures, assuring the timid, distributing encouragement and endearment to all" (Mann, 1844a, p. 134). As with Pestalozzi, it was not simply about the transmission of knowledge but rather about empathy, so that book knowledge was deemed comparatively unimportant: "But the Prussian teacher has no book. He needs none. He teaches from a full mind" (Mann, 1844a, p. 123). The effect was, as with Pestalozzi, reflected morality: "In the mean time, the children are delighted. Their perceptive powers are exercised. Their reflecting faculties are developed. Their moral sentiments are cultivated" (Mann, 1844a, p. 123). It is merely logical that during his visits, Mann never wanted to notice any cases of disciplining (p. 133).

Passages such as these in Mann's report show clearly what the experts from other countries were interested in. They were not simply looking for a specific best practice that they would describe and then implement at home. Rather, they "described" ideal practice that they believed or purported to observe abroad. They were abroad on a mission for their own fatherland, which in the case of United States was undergoing at the time a process of nationalization after the nearly three years of war between the United States and England (1812–1815). The epoch is called the "Era of Good Feelings"[2] (Dangerfield, 1952) and is closely associated with the presidency of James Monroe,[3] who tried to achieve national unity by eliminating political parties (Unger, 2009). But in a way that was similar to Europe, the process of national unity—and thus the drawing of a line of demarcation between one's own country and others, the most remarkable expression of which was the Monroe Doctrine of 1823[4]—was tied up with processes of education, with the aim to "transform children into citizens of a particular kind" (Tröhler, Popkewitz, and Labaree, 2011, p. 1). On both sides of the Atlantic, the defined nation had to be stabilized through educated citizens. This triggered an enormous need for reform, which in turn created the demand for advocates and experts in this reform—in the United States people like Mann and Barnard and others.

12.2 Influence, reception, effect

With the defeat of Napoleon, Napoleon's Continental System against England also fell in 1814, which brought not only cheap merchandise to continental Europe but also people with ideas and interests. Due to the circumstance that Napoleon's rule had not changed England's territory, England was not faced with the task of developing a program of nation building, especially as it had no constitution that set out the task of educating citizens. Accordingly, there was no widespread mass education movement that would have needed role models like Pestalozzi. In this respect the English Pestalozzians were restricted to the field of education for the poor, which had been initiated by numerous religious individuals and groups.

A typical example here is William Allen (1770–1843), son of an English silk producer, who was a pharmacist and chemist and the head of a famous pharmaceutical company. As a Quaker and a philanthropist (whereby he particularly made a name for himself as an opponent of slavery) Allen was interested in educational issues. While on a mission trip to Europe of several years, he visited Pestalozzi in Yverdon. He then founded a Quaker school for girls in Stoke Newington (today a part of

London) in 1824, which he directed up to 1838. Another example is the Irishman John Synge (1788–1845) who traveled Europe in 1814 and also visited Pestalozzi in Yverdon. After his return to Ireland, he founded his own institute in Roundwood (County Wicklow) and wrote publications on Pestalozzi to disseminate the Pestalozzi method to English speakers. But the most famous of the English Pestalozzians was Charles Mayo (1792–1846),[5] who was ordained in 1817 and was the headmaster of the high school in Bridgnorth, Shropshire. Mayo came to hear of Pestalozzi from his close friend John Synge. In 1819 he gave up his post as headmaster and went to Yverdon, where he stayed for three years and supervised the "English colony," the many English students at the institute at the time. Returning to England in 1822, Mayo was an enthusiastic promoter of Pestalozzi's educational method. To this purpose he opened his own model school in Epsom, Surrey, which in 1826 was moved to Cheam near London to accommodate the great number of applicants. All of these English activities remained private initiatives, often religiously motivated, for there was no program of state-funded schools for the public for many years to come. The activities thus came to a halt when the persons responsible became old or died.

Things were completely different in the United States, which had to reinvent itself territorially several times and also, at least as a basic idea, was bound by a program of citizenship education. From 1815 to 1828, an era that Dangerfield (1965) called the "awakening of American nationalism," was also the period of another movement also called an awakening—namely, the Second Great Awakening, a widespread religious movement within Protestantism that had begun shortly before 1800, was very widespread by 1820, and reached its high point in the 1840s, mainly in New England. Many of the converts believed that their movement heralded the Second Coming of Jesus Christ, and they were responsible for innumerable reforms that aimed at remedying social wrongs (Smith, 1957). A very central reform was comprehensive school reform, for the educational turn was after all in its essence a Protestant reaction to the changes in a society undergoing transformation, changes which in the United States in particular were also connected with the massive development of the transportation system (the Erie Canal was opened in 1815 and completely transformed the State of New York and especially Rochester[6]). These transformations caused uncertainties to which the response was—in the sense of the educational turn—educational concepts. This is clearly illustrated by a book by Edward

Deering Mansfield (1801–1880)[7], jurist and publicist, who without preliminary study published *American Education, its Principles and Elements: Dedicated to the Teachers of the United States* (Mansfield, 1851), in which he stated bluntly: "in this period of rapid development" the task was to determine "ideas connected with a republican and Christian education" and in this connection to focus on the "*entire soul*" (p. vii).

Protestant visions of redemption, American nationalism, and educational reform went hand in hand in this period of great societal transformation. This is shown clearly by the most successful textbook, alongside the Bible and *Webster's Dictionary*, of the nineteenth century—namely, the *McGuffey Readers*,[8] published starting in 1836. According to Skrabec (2009), the *McGuffey Readers*:

> hailed American exceptionalism, manifest destiny, and America as God's country...Critics see the patriotism of McGuffey as extreme nationalism. Certainly, McGuffey and many of his readers truly believed America superior to other nations. Furthermore, McGuffey saw America as having a future mission to bring liberty and democracy to the world. (p. 223)

There is no mistake about the Protestant idea of redemption behind this agenda; after all, the publisher of the *McGuffey Readers* was William Holmes McGuffey (1800–1873), the son of a Scottish immigrant and an ordained Presbyterian minister. McGuffey was evidently—at least in part—inspired by Pestalozzi's educational approach (see Skrabec, 2009, pp. 175f.). Upon this background, it is no coincidence that in addition to a religious and a national awakening, there was also a "Great Educational Awakening" that George Campbell Hage even described as the "offshoot" of the Second Great Awakening (Hage, n.d., p. 5). And Barlow (1977) concluded that the Great Educational Awakening was connected with "an upsurge of Pestalozzianism" (p. 86).

This raises the question as to whether and how Pestalozzi had an influence—direct or indirect—on the shaping of the school system on both sides of the Atlantic. According to Skrabec, a William McGuffey researcher, Pestalozzi had much less influence than that ascribed to him by older research (Skrabec, 2009): "The Pestalozzi methodology was in vogue in the 1830s. The point is that Pestalozzi is long forgotten, while McGuffey remains a well-recognized figure" (p. 176). This stands in marked contrast to assessments by Paul Monroe, for instance, the famous historian of education at Columbia University, who noted that Mann's well-known *Seventh Annual Report* (Mann, 1844) was "the most important single influence in spreading Pestalozzian ideas of method, discipline, school management, and curriculum throughout the United States" (Monroe, 1940, p. 384). Which opinion is correct?

As noted at the beginning of this book, Pestalozzi did not invent the modern school. Monroe's statement that "Pestalozzian ideas of method, discipline, school management, and curriculum" were disseminated in the United States by Mann's report cannot be correct, not only because Pestalozzi is not even named in Mann's report but also because Pestalozzi never said anything about "discipline, school management, and curriculum" that was compatible with and applicable in the nineteenth century. As for the other position, Skrabec's (2009) comment that "Pestalozzi is long forgotten, while McGuffey remains a well-recognized figure" (p. 176) not only is factually wrong (it is at best an expression of the American nationalism that Skrabec describes in his book) but also fails to recognize the historiographical problem of the distinction between influence, reception, and effect.

The term influence is highly disputed as a historiographical category. The French intellectual Lucien Goldmann, for example, wrote that alleged influences "explain little, if anything, in intellectual history" (Goldmann, 1969, p. 92)—not to mention Foucault's criticism of the idea of historical linearity, that is, continuity through influence (Foucault, 1973, p. 23). Less radical but equally critical is Cambridge historian Quentin Skinner's declaration that most historiographies designed as linear sequence of influences are "purely mythological." *Prior* to the assertion of the one or the other influence, Skinner demands thorough examination of three "necessary conditions:" first, whether an allegedly influenced writer has actually read the texts that allegedly influenced him; second, whether the writer could have acquired the insights only from those texts and not from other sources; third, whether he could not have come to the insights on his own (Skinner 1988, p. 46f.; Skinner 2002a, p. 75f.).

The first condition, reception, can be examined through laborious reconstruction of publications, (private) archives, and (private) libraries, but the second condition is almost impossible to examine in a booming market of educational publications, and the third condition is often examined merely in the form of speculation in the service of certain interests (as in the case of Skrabec, 2009, p. 176). If reconstructing reception is possible but extremely laborious and primarily pays off the effort constructing hagiographies, and if influence can hardly be determined, then there remains only the idea of effect, which, however, does *not* have to be understood as the consequence of reception. Effects occur also without explicit reception—that is, through cultural socialization. For example, values that many people in the Western world share, and ways in which they act, are expression of the history of the impact of the Bible—without them necessarily having ever read the Bible. We thus speak of shared values that also without explicit reading are transmitted from generation to generation and build a stable cultural system that even—at least in the belief of Protestants—does without institutions altogether: it is no coincidence that the Chicago pragmatists John Dewey, George Herbert Mead, and James Hayden Tufts, whose parents were socialized in New England in the 1840s and 1850s at the high point of the Second Great Awakening, developed an educational theory around 1900 in the context of their democratic ideas, ideas that were strongly colored by Protestant Congregationalism and that therefore accordingly marginalized institutions (Tröhler, 2006).

12.3 Pestalozzi and the moral discourse of teacher education in the United States

Upon this background, then, the question concerning Pestalozzi's influence or his indirect (based on reception) effect does not play a very important role. It seems more important to examine what role Pestalozzi has in the discourse that in the early nineteenth century became manifest as the educationalization of social problems. It is very evident that teacher education was of the greatest interest here, because a professional group needed to be trained that could implement the program of the educational turn. And it is upon this background that the great interest in teacher education on the part of the American visitors to Germany should be understood. It should be taken into account that in contrast to today, prospective teachers did not usually have an academic diploma or degree. The German university entry qualification, the *Abitur*, or a high school diploma were not required for admission to a "teacher seminar" or a "normal school," as these early schools or colleges for the training of teachers were called. To be a teacher meant—and the religious expression is not by chance—"first, a deep sense of being 'called' to serve...: The desire to produce teachers who possessed these characteristics was the central motive of the normal school and the definitive element in what was later called the 'teachers college slant'" (Borrowman, 1965, p. 34).

For this commitment on the part of the teachers, History of Education was introduced as a college subject in its own right and was systematically developed in Germany following Germany's victory in the Franco-Prussian War in 1871 (in this war, under Prussia's leadership, Germany became unified as an empire). For the purposes of nation building the school system was greatly expanded, and teachers were given far better training, and for this History of Education was developed to provide teachers with a moral and national education. France, Germany's recent enemy, copied this model a short time later, adapting it to its own national requirements, and from there it found its way to the United States, in part via translations (see, for example, Compayré's (1888) *The History of Pedagogy*) and in part via original publications.

In this moralizing discourse of the educational turn, Pestalozzi took the prominent position. Based on that, the erroneous conclusion was drawn that Pestalozzi had founded the modern school or at least made the modern school possible. The admiration for the synthesis of moral-religious empathy and dedication in the teaching profession began with the earliest Histories of Education. In *History and Progress of Education: From the Earliest Times to the Present. Intended as a Manual for Teachers and Students*, for which Henry Barnard wrote the foreword, Linus Pierpont Brockett, the son of a Baptist preacher, wrote (under the pseudonym Philobiblius) the following about Pestalozzi:

> The man who has exerted the most influence over the education of the race, in the last hundred years, is J. H. Pestalozzi...a man of warm and loving heart, of high and pure aspirations, and of a deeply religious spirit. (Brockett, 1859, p. 241)

Twenty years later, Franklin Verzelius Newton Painter, a Lutheran clergyman, reiterated in *A History of Education* (Painter, 1886):

> Pestalozzi. At the threshold of this century stands an educator who commands both our admiration and love. In the long line of educational reformers since the Reformation there is perhaps no other that has done so much for popular education. The devotion of his life, as well as the truth of his pedagogic principles, has been a power in the educational world.... Following the example of our divine Master, he gave himself for the good of others. (pp. 266f.)

And only a few years later, William J. Shoup, a theologian in the Old German Baptist Brethren Church, wrote the following in *The History* and *Science of Education: For Institutes, Normal Schools, Reading Circles and Private Self-Instruction of Teachers* (Shoup, 1891): "In 1746, Pestalozzi, the most famous of educational reformers was born at Zurich...First among the causes of his popularity is the genuine, unselfish goodness of the man" (pp. 227f.).

The success of the moral educationalization in the context of teacher education would bear fruit. Levi Seeley, who was an alumnus of the Normal School in Albany (New York) but also received an M.A. degree at Williams College and completed a PhD at the University of Leipzig from 1883 to 1886, wrote in *History of Education* (Seeley, 1899):

> But the greatest lesson that Pestalozzi taught is embodied in the word *love*. He loved little children, he loved the distressed and lowly, he loved all this fellow-men. By the spirit which actuated him, by the methods of instruction employed, by a life of disappointment and apparent failure, by the appreciation of his service after he had gone to his rest, by the accelerated growth of his teachings throughout the world, he more closely resembles the Great Teacher than any other man that has ever lived. (p. 271)

Around 1900, Pestalozzi was the hero of historiography, the man who through his love and dedication had left such a strong mark on the modern school that he was chosen to be the father of modern education-chosen, for example, by Thomas Davidson, a philosopher of Scottish descent, who wrote in *A History of Education* (Davidson, 1901):

> The first man who took a notable step forward in education, on the lines of Rousseau and Kant—that is, toward Nature and Reason, was Pestalozzi...With little learning, and less system, but with overwhelming faith in the people and love for children, this warm-hearted, devoted man may fairly be said to be the father of modern popular education. (pp. 229f.)

And when, a few years later, Monroe (1908) quite rightly warned against a "common error to overestimate the importance of this one reformer in the history of education," in the same breath he also stated in the style of progressive education that he saw in Pestalozzi "the germs of modern educational ideas" (p. 308)—namely, child-centered education: "He it was who first made clear and forced upon the public the position that the whole problem of education was to be considered from the point of view of developing mind of the child" (p. 308).

These histories prove to be less than historiographies in the modern sense of the term, meaning reconstruction of past developments. Instead, they affirmed the discursive trope that the genre History of Education created in the first place: the all-encompassing educationalization of social problems, the associated expansion of the school system, and the resulting need for professionalization of teachers, who were supposed to stand out with their empathy and commitment and for whose training and preparation (among other reasons) the subject History of Education was developed. The histories did not serve clarification of past facts or of the prehistory of the present day but instead served as compilations of examples and role models to emulate. Pestalozzi, as "the father of modern popular education," was the most shining example, and on this basis he could quite easily be turned into the "founder of the modern public school."

With this, the school was (and probably today still feels the effects) an institution for moral education in a culture that had more difficulty coming to terms with its progress than might have been necessary. What did Horace Mann say in a lecture in 1840 about the diverse economic and social developments?

> Now the simple question for an American, is, whether all this mighty accession of power, growing out of our free institutions, shall or shall not be placed in the hands of these ravenous and tyrannizing propensities.... If the propensities are to prevail, then speculation will supersede industry; violence will usurp the prerogatives of the law; the witness will be perjured upon jurors; and the guilty be rescued by forsworn jurors. (Mann, 1845, p. 170)

In this educationalized culture, the recipe for dealing with the dangers looming on all sides could only be education of the whole person, encompassing (as Pestalozzi so frequently stressed) the head, the heart, and the hand: "The world is to be rescued through physical, intellectual, moral and religious action upon the young" (Mann, 1845, p. 172).

12.4 History, education, and redemption

In today's discussions, especially in news coverage expressing opinions on the current situation of the world, the question is often raised as to whether—given world hunger, human trafficking, and social injustices—we can in fact call ourselves the heirs of the Enlightenment, which in the eighteenth century brought forth the notions of equality, human rights, and progress for the common welfare. Upon this background of postmodern skepticism, Darnton (1997) suggested that we define the Enlightenment clearly, historically and geographically, as follows: the French discussion in and after the mid-eighteenth century. With this, we can distinguish the different national reform discussions of the eighteenth century and also disburden the French Enlightenment discussion from the later developments—for instance, that the terrible events in the twentieth century are, to some extent, direct consequences of the Enlightenment attempts to rationalize the world by virtue of reason and science.

To what extent we may view ourselves as heirs of the Enlightenment—or more precisely, as heirs of the diverse reform discussions that are grouped together under the collective term "the Enlightenment"—and to what extent postmodern criticism is sustainable must remain unanswered for now. But it is certain that there exists a discursive *topos* to which most of the postmodernists are indebted and which arose in the 50 years before and after 1800. This discursive topos is not identical to that which is understood as "Enlightenment." On the contrary, it is characterized by criticism of the Enlightenment and, in Lutheran Germany, even by Pietism. It is the discursive *topos* of the educationalization of social problems—that is, the interpretation of perceived problems *as educational problems*. Shortly before 1800, fear of corruption of the soul in the context of economic development had created this *topos* in Reformed Protestant republicanism, which in Lutheran Germany even took on not-worldly or spiritual forms, and the task of nation building was tied to the expansion of the education systems, which needed teachers who were to implement the creation of the nation. Teacher education needed moral guides, and teachers needed role models to identify with and with whom they could establish themselves as a professional group. Pestalozzi was the ideal person to fill both roles during his lifetime and throughout the nineteenth century.

Although later his name was used less and less often and his direct influence on the school was deemed less irrefutable, Pestalozzi remains the personified figurehead of this educational turn, which not only continued uninterruptedly but also was steadily expanded. When in 1957 during the Cold War the Soviet Union's launching of the manmade satellite Sputnik caused great uncertainty among Americans, teachers were blamed for putting Americans at a disadvantage in the international competition for technological advances. The result was the *National Defense Education Act* of 1958 (Tröhler, 2010). And in 1960, when the aim was to protect the Mediterranean countries from communism, the Organization for Economic Cooperation and Development (OECD) developed the Mediterranean Regional Project (MRP), which was intended to transform the predominantly agricultural economies in Portugal, Spain, Italy, Yugoslavia, Greece, and Turkey into industrial economies via expansion of the education system (Tröhler, in press). And in the same educationalizing genre, Paul Wolfowitz, president of the World Bank at the time, wrote in 2007:

> The time has never been better to invest in young people living in developing countries—that is the message of this year's World Development Report... The number of people worldwide aged 12–24 years has reached 1.3 billion, the largest in history. It is also the healthiest and best educated—a strong base to build on in a world that demands more than basic skills. Today's youth are tomorrow's workers, entrepreneurs, parents, active citizens, and, indeed, leaders.... Investing in young people strongly contributes to the Bank's overarching mission of fighting poverty. At the same time, investing in young people is a challenge for governments in all countries, rich and poor. (Wolfowitz, 2007, p. xi)

Pestalozzi was not the founder of this cultural reflex to frame social problems as education problems, but he grew up in the environment in which this tendency came into being, and due to a combination of his personal traits and outstanding qualities he was able to make precisely those promises that promised new assurance and security to countries on both sides of the Atlantic that had been made fundamentally uncertain by modernization developments and that were war-weary after the Napoleonic events. The fact that Pestalozzi in his person could link the cultural demands for security in the encompassing transformations of his time in the direction of an open future—that is, the promises of "the method" as educational tool in an educationalized culture—with Christian ethics of dedication made him credible far and wide. On the basis of the certainty of Christian ethics, any specific educational model was beyond criticism. When the model was institutionalized with the establishment of the modern public school and with teacher education, it still needed Pestalozzi in the medium term as a guarantor and for self-reassurance. Later, it needed Pestalozzi less and less. The model had become independent, and towards the end of the nineteenth century it had also broken through the boundaries of Protestantism, and (much later) it also manifested itself outside Christian contexts.

Anyone wanting to understand what education and the schools mean today has to understand how they *became* that which they represent today, what the expectations were of them, and what secular notions of redemption were connected with them, and would do well to study Pestalozzi. Not because he founded the modern public school—this would be simply a historical fact (if it were true)—but rather because he decisively shaped and reinforced a discursive *topos* that is still incredibly pervasive today and from which we can partly emancipate ourselves only through historical reconstruction. This, finally, makes history a form of enlightenment, for:

> Without understanding the history and interests of our sciences, we become trapped by our metaphors and limit our possibilities. (Popkewitz, 1984, p. 151)

And, as Quentin Skinner put it, we have to make use of the opportunity in "that historical study [has] the power to transform us, to help us think more effectively about our society and its possible need for reform and reformation" (Skinner, 2002b, p. 26), because "to learn from the past... is to learn one of the keys to self-awareness itself" (Skinner 2002a, p. 89). In education, Pestalozzi is one of the cornerstones, if not *the* cornerstone, for an awareness of ourselves in our discursive materialization of the educational reflex.

Notes

1. The progressive reformers in Prussia were national—that is, in Fichte's sense oriented towards to entire German-speaking territory and thus not restricted only to the Kingdom of Prussia—and they were thought to be relatively liberal. The murder in 1819 of a conservative playwright named August von Kotzebue by a liberal (in the Prussian sense) but militant nationalist was sufficient provocation for the reactionaries to put a stop to all of the reforms; see http://en.wikipedia.org/wiki/August_von_Kotzebue
2. http://en.wikipedia.org/wiki/Era_of_Good_Feelings
3. http://en.wikipedia.org/wiki/James_Monroe
4. http://en.wikipedia.org/wiki/Monroe_Doctrine
5. http://en.wikisource.org/wiki/Mayo,_Charles_(1792–1846)_(DNB00)
6. An outstanding description of the social consequences of the new transportation system and the subsequent evangelical reactions in the context of the Second Great Awakening is provided by Paul E. Johnson

in *A Shopkeeper's Millennium: Society and Revivals in Rochester* (Johnson, 1978). Germany's very different, almost opposite reaction to comparable developments is described by Tröhler (2010a).
7   http://en.wikipedia.org/wiki/Edward_Deering_Mansfield
8   http://en.wikipedia.org/wiki/McGuffey_Readers

References

Association of Masters of the Boston Public School. (1844). *Remarks on the Seventh Annual Report of the Hon. Horace Mann, Secretary of the Massachusetts Board of Education.* Boston, MA: C.C. Little and J. Brown.

Auszug aus einem Brief aus der Schweiz. (1801). *Der Neue Teutsche Merkur,* 2, 158-160.

Bailyn, B. (1993) (ed.). *The Debate on the Constitution: Federalists and Antifederalist Speeches, Articles, and Letters during the Struggle over Ratification.* New York, NY: Library of America.

Barlow, T. A. (1977). *Pestalozzi and American Education.* Boulder, CO: Este Es Press (University of Colorado Libraries).

Barnard, H. (1851). *Normal Schools and Other Institutions, Agencies, and Means Designed for the Professional Education of Teachers.* Hartford, CT: Case, Tiffany and Company.

Barnard, H. (1854). *National Education in Europe Being an Account of the Organization, Administration, Instruction, and Statistics of Public Schools of Different Grades in the Principle States.* New York, NY: Norton.

Biber, E. (1827). *Beitrag zur Biographie Heinrich Pestalozzi's und zur Beleuchtung seiner neuesten Schrift "Meine Lebensschicksale u. s. f.".* St Gallen, Switzerland: Bei Wegelin und Rätzer.

Biber, E. (1830). *Christian Education in a Course of Lectures Delivered in London in Spring 1828.* London, UK: Effingham Wilson

Biber, E. (1831). *Henry Pestalozzi and His Plan of Education: Being an Account of His Life and Writings with Copious*

Extracta from His Works and Extensive Details Illustrative of the Practical Parts of His Method. London, UK: John Souter.

Biester, J. E. (1804). Einleitung und Kommentar zu: Riemann, Karl Friedrich 1804. *Neue Berlinische Monatsschrift*, 1, 122–123, 137–146.

Borrowman, M. L. (1965). *Teacher Education in America: A Documentary History*. New York, NY: Teachers College Press.

Brockett, L. P. (pseud. Philobiblius). (1859). *History and Progress of Education, from the Earliest Times to the Present: Intended as a Manual for Teachers and Students*. New York, NY: A.S. Barnes & Burr.

Bündnis der vereinigten Staaten in America. (1777). Hamphsire, Massachusetsbay, Rhodeisland, Connecticut, Neuyorc, Pensilvanien, der Grafschaften Neucastle, Kent und Sussex an der Delaware, Maryland, Virginien, die zwei Carolina und Georgien. Vom vierten Chrsitmonats 1776. *Ephemeriden der Menschheit*, 2(6), 320–332.

Cajot, D. J. B. (1766). *Les plagiats de M. J.J. R. de Genève, sur l'éducation*. Paris, France: Durant.

Caluori, B., Horlacher, R., and Tröhler, D. (2012). Publizieren als Netzwerkstrategie: Die Gesamtausgabe der Werke Pestalozzis bei Cotta. *Zeitschrift für Pädagogik*, 58, 877–897.

Compayré, G. (1888). *History of Pedagogy. Translated, with an Introduction, Notes, and an Index by W.H. Payne*. Boston, MA: D.C. Heath & Co. (Original work published 1883)

Condorcet, M. J. A. N. de (1795 [1796; English]). *Outlines of an Historical View of the Progress of the Human Mind*, being a posthumous work of the late M. de Condorcet. Philadelphia, PA: Printed by Lang and Ustick for M. Carey, H. & P. Rice & Co., J. Ormrod, B.F. Bache, and J. Fellows, New-York. (Original work published in French 1795)

Cousin, V. (1832). *Rapport sur l'état de l'instruction publique dans quelques pays de l'Allemagne, et particulièrement en Prusse*. Paris, France: Imprimerie royale.

Cousin, V. (1835). *Report on the State of Public Instruction in Prussia; Addressed to the Count de Montalivet. With Plans of School Houses*. New York, NY: Wiley & Long.

Dangerfield, G. (1952). *The Era of Good Feelings*. New York, NY: Harcourt, Brace.

Dangerfield, G. (1965). *The Awakening of American Nationalism: 1815–1828*. New York, NY: Harper and Row.

Darnton, R. (1997). George Washington's false teeth. *The New York Review of Books*, 44(5), 34-38.

Dash, M. (1999). *Tulipomania: The Story of the World's most Coveted Flower and the Extraordinary Passions it Aroused.* London, UK: Gollancz.

Davidson, T. (1901). *A History of Education.* New York, NY: Charles Scribner's Sons.

De Guimps, R. (2004). *Pestalozzi: His Life and Work* (J. Russell, trans.). New York, NY: Adamant Media Corporation. Elibron Classics. (Translation first published 1890)

DeJean, J. (1997). *Ancients Against Moderns: Culture Wars and the Making of a Fin de Siecle.* Chicago, IL: University Of Chicago Press.

Dejung, E. (1976). Entgegnung auf Eduard Bibers Buch. In A. Buchenau, E. Spranger, and H. Stettbacher (eds), *Pestalozzis Sämtliche Werke, Volume 28* (pp. 482-499). Berlin, Germany: Walter de Gruyter.

de L'Aspée, H. (1865). *Calisthenics; or the Elements of Bodily Culture on Pestalozzian Principles: Designed for Practical Education in Schools, Colleges, Families etc.* London, UK: Griffin.

de Rougement, G. (2010). Rougemont an Pestalozzi vom 18. Mai 1808. In R. Horlacher and D. Tröhler (eds), *Sämtliche Briefe an Pestalozzi, Volume II* (pp. 478–479). Zurich, Switzerland: NZZ Libro. (written 1808)

Dewey, J. (1915). *German Philosophy and Politics.* New York, NY: Holt and Company.

Dickson, P. G. M. (1970). *The Financial Revolution in England: A Study in the Development of Public Credit, 1688-1756.* Aldershot, UK: Gregg Revivals.

Diesterweg, A. W. (1828). Bemerkungen über den Rechenunterricht, mit besonderer Beziehung auf das praktische Rechenbuch von Diesterweg und Heuser. *Rheinische Blätter für Erziehung und Unterricht*, 3(3), 86-101.

Diesterweg, A. W. (1829). Der jetzige Standpunkt der Pestalozzi'schen Schule, und das Treiben der After-Pestalozzianer unserer Zeit. *Rheinische Blätter für Erziehung und Unterricht*, 4, 455-484.

Diesterweg, A. W., Kalisch, E. W., and Massmann, H. F. (1845). *Die Feier des 100sten Geburtstages Heinrich Pestalozzi's in Berlin am 12. Januar 1845: Vorfeier des hundertjährigen Jubiläums seiner Geburt am 12. Januar 1846; Aufruf zur Theilnahme an einer zu Pestalozzi's Gedächtniss, nach seinen Grundsätzen und Absichten zu errichtenden landwirthschaftlichen*

Armenanstalt – eines "Neuhofs" – als Musteranstalt für Waisenerziehung. Berlin, Germany: Vossische Buchhandlung.

Diesterweg, A. W. (1845). *Heinrich Pestalozzi: ein Wort über ihn und seine unsterblichen Verdienste, für die Kinder und deren Eltern, zu dem ersten Säcularfeste seiner Geburt.* Berlin, Germany: Enslin.

Diesterweg, A. W. (1846). *Heinrich Pestalozzi : Rede bei der Männer-Feier seines hundertjährigen Geburtstages am 12. Januar 1846 in Berlin.* Berlin, Germany: Enslin.

Englische Kolonien in Amerika. Kundmachung ihrer Trennung von Engelland. Batrachtung über die Freyheit. (1776). *Ephemeriden der Menschheit*, 1(9), 82–92.

Entwurf der pensylvanischen Regierungsform. (1777). *Ephemeriden der Menschheit*, 2(1), 80–94.

Erziehungsrat Luzern. (2009). Erziehungsrat Luzern an Pestalozzi vom 11. Mai 1803. In R. Horlacher and D. Tröhler (eds), *Sämtliche Briefe an Pestalozzi, Band I* (pp. 593–595). Zurich, Switzerland: Nzz Libro. (Written 1803)

Ewald, J. L. (2009). Ewald an Pestalozzi vom 29. Mai 1803. In R. Horlacher and D. Tröhler (eds), *Sämtliche Briefe an Pestalozzi, Band I* (pp. 596–599). Zurich, Switzerland, NZZ Libro. (Written 1803)

Fichte, J. G. (1793). *Beitrag zur Berichtigung der Urtheile des Publikums über die französische Revolution.* Danzig, Germany.

Fichte, J. G. (1808). *Reden an die deutsche Nation.* Berlin, Germany: Realschulbuchhandlung.

Fichte, J. G. (2008). *Addresses to the German nation* (G. Moore, trans. and ed.), Cambridge, UK: Cambridge University Press. (Original work published 1808)

Foucault M. (1973). *Archäologie des Wissens.* Frankfurt/M., Germany: Suhrkamp. (Original work published 1969)

Fröbel, F. W. A. (2010). Fröbel an Pestalozzi vom 8. Juli 1808. In R. Horlacher and D. Tröhler (eds), *Sämtliche Briefe an Pestalozzi, Volume II* (pp. 507–518). Zurich, Switzerland: NZZ Libro. (Written 1808)

Fuseli, H. [Füssli, H.] (1767). *Remarks on the Writings and Conduct of J. J. Rousseau.* London, UK: Printed for T. Cadell, J. Johnson and B. Davenport, and J. Payne.

Girard, G., Merian, A. and Trechsel, F. (1810). *Bericht über die Pestalozzische Erziehungs-Anstalt zu Yverdon an Seine Excellenz den Herrn Landammann und die Hohe Tagsatzung der Schweizerischen Eydgenossenschaft.* Bern, Switzerland: Haller.

Godenzi. L. (2012). Das Zürcher Privatschulwesen (1800–1820). *Bildungsgeschichte, International Journal fort the Historiography of Education*, 2(2), 176–192.

Goldmann, L. (1969). *The Human Sciences & Philosophy* (H. V. White and R. Anchor, trans.). London, UK: Cape. (Original work published 1952)

Graber, R. (1993). *Bürgerliche Öffentlichkeit und spätabsolutistischer Staat: Sozietätenbewegung und Konfliktkonjunktur in Zürich 1746–1780* [Bourgeois Public and Late Absolutist State: Societies Movement and High Point of Conflict in Zurich, 1746–1780]. Zurich, Switzerland: Chronos.

Grundsätze, nach welchem die an dem Delaware Flusse gelegenen englischen Colonien ihre Verfassung einzurichten beschlossen haben. 11. Herbstmonat 1776. (1777). *Ephemeriden der Menschheit*, 2(4), 109–114.

GutsMuths, J. C. F. (1800). An den verehrten Leser. *Bibliothek der pädagogischen Literatur*, 1, 1–14.

Hage, G. C. (n.d.). *Horace Mann's Cultural and Educational Proposal of the Emergence of the New Adam and the New Creation of God: A Study of Cultural Conflict and Change in United States History*. http://www.drginnc.com/upload/Horace%20Mann%27s%20Proposal,%201.pdf

Herbart, J. F. (1802). *Pestalozzi's Idee eines ABC der Anschauung*. Götttingen, Germany: Röwer.

Himly, J. F. W. (1803). *Versuch einer Einleitung in die Grundsätze des Pestalozzi'schen Elementar-Unterrichts*. Berlin, Germany: Haude und Spener.

Hirschman, A. O. (1977). *The Passions and the Interests: Political Arguments for Capitalism before Its Triumph*. Princeton, NJ: Princeton University Press.

Holzhey, H., and Zurbuchen, S. (1997). *Alte Löcher – neue Blicke: Zürich im 18. Jahrhundert*. Zurich, Switzerland: Chronos.

Horlacher, R. (2011). "Best practice" around 1800: Johann Heinrich Pestalozzi's educational enterprise in Switzerland and the establishment of private Pestalozzi schools abroad. *Encounters on Education*, 12, 3–17.

Horlacher, R. (2012). What is *Bildung*? Or: Why *Pädagogik* cannot get away from the concept of *Bildung*. In P. Siljander, A. Kivelä, and A. Sutinen (eds), *Theories of Bildung and Growth: Connections and Controversies between Continental Educational Thinking and American*

Pragmatism (pp. 135-147). Rotterdam, The Netherlands: Sense Publishers.

Horlacher, R. (2013). Standardisierung durch Vorbilder? Das Beispiel Pestalozzi. *Bildungsgeschichte. International Journal for the Historiography of Education*, 3(1), 20-35.

Iselin, I. (1781). Schreiben eines Vaters an seinen Sohn, der sich der Handelschaft widmet [Letter of a father to his son, on the subject of trade]. *Ephemeriden der Menschheit oder Bibliothek der Sittenlehre, der Politik, und der Gesetzgebung*, 9, 385-425.

Ith, J. S. (1802). *Amtlicher Bericht über die Pestalozzische Anstalt und die neue Lehrart desselben*. Bern, Switzerland: H. Gessner.

Jacobi, F. H. (2009). Brief an Pestalozzi 24. März 1794 [Letter to Pestalozzi 24 March 1794]. In R. Horlacher and D. Tröhler (eds), *Sämtliche Briefe an Pestalozzi, Volume 1* (pp. 276-279). Zurich, Switzerland: NZZ Libro. (Written 1794)

Jefferson, T. (1984). Notes on the State of Virginia. In M. D. Peterson (ed.), *Thomas Jefferson: Writings* (pp. 123-325). New York, NY: Literary Classics of the United States. (First published 1785, 1787)

Jeismann, K.-E. (1995). American observations concerning the Prussian educational system in the nineteenth century. In H. Geitz, J. Heideking, and J. Herbst (eds), *German Influences on Education in the United States* (pp. 21-41). Cambridge, UK: Cambridge University Press.

Johnson, P. E. (1978). *A Shopkeeper's Millennium: Society and Revivals in Rochester*. New York, NY: Hill and Wang.

Kasthofer, R. (in press/1827). Brief an Pestalozzi vom 17. Februar 1827 [Letter to Pestalozzi 17 February 1827]. In R. Horlacher and D. Tröhler (eds), *Sämtliche Briefe an Pestalozzi, Volume 6*. Zurich, Switzerland: NZZ Libro.

Kleiner Rat von Bern. (2010). Kleiner Rat von Bern an Pestalozzi vom 22. Februar 1804. In R. Horlacher and D. Tröhler (eds), *Sämtliche Briefe an Pestalozzi, Volume I* (pp. 691-692). Zurich, Switzerland: Nzz Libro. (Written 1804)

Kohlrausch, F. (1814). *Deutschlands Zukunft. In sechs Reden* [*The Future of Germany. In Six Talks*]. Elberfeld, Germany: Heinrich Büschler.

Kohlrausch, F. (2012). Brief an Pestalozzi 9. April 1814 [Letter to Pestalozzi 9 April 1814]. In R. Horlacher and D. Tröhler (eds), *Sämtliche Briefe an Pestalozzi, Volume 4* (pp. 52-54). Zurich, Switzerland: NZZ Libro. (Written 1814)

König Christian VII. (2009). *König Christian VII von Dänemark an Pestalozzi vom 20. November 1802*. In R. Horlacher and D. Tröhler (eds), *Sämtliche Briefe an Pestalozzi, Volume I* (pp. 565-568). Zurich, Switzerland: NZZ Libro. (Written 1802)

Krüsi, H. (2010). *Brief an Pestalozzi vom 20. September 1808*. In R. Horlacher and D. Tröhler (eds), *Sämtliche Briefe an Pestalozzi, Volume 2* (pp. 559-560). Zurich, Switzerland: NZZ Libro. (Written 1808)

Ladomus, Johann Jakob Friedrich (2010). *Ladomus an Pestalozzi vom 11. Juni 1808*. In R. Horlacher and D. Tröhler (eds), *Sämtliche Briefe an Pestalozzi, Volume II* (pp. 487-490). Zurich, Switzerland: Nzz Libro. (Written 1808)

Le Goff, J. (1956). *Marchands et banquiers au Moyen âge*. Paris, France: Presses universitaires de France.

Le Goff, J. (1986). *La Bourse et la vie: économie et religion au Moyen âge*. Paris, France: Hachette.

Lehr, F. (2010). *Lehr an Pestalozzi vom 1. November 1808*. In R. Horlacher and D. Tröhler (eds), *Sämtliche Briefe an Pestalozzi, Volume II* (pp. 600-601). Zürich, Switzerland: Nzz Libro. (Written 1808)

Leyden, F. A. van. (2010). *Leyden an Pestalozzi vom 12. September 1808*. In R. Horlacher and D. Tröhler (eds), *Sämtliche Briefe an Pestalozzi, Volume II* (pp. 546-548). Zürich, Switzerland: Nzz Libro. (Written 1808)

Luginbühl, R. (1902). *Philipp Albert Stapfer, helvetischer Minister der Künste und Wissenschaften (1766-1840)* [*Philipp Albert Stapfer, Helvetic Minister of the Arts and Sciences (1766-1840)*]. Basel, Switzerland: R. Reich.

Lutz, L. (1930). Brief an Anton Gruner. *Pestalozzianum, 27*, 1-2. (Written 1804)

Mably, G. B. de (1763). *Entretiens de Phocion: sur le rapport de la morale avec la politique / trad. en grec de Nicoclès; avec des remarques*. Amsterdam, The Netherlands.

Mably, G. B. de (1764). *Gespräche des Phocion über die Beziehung der Morale mit der Polititk. Aus dem Griechischen des Nicocles. Mit Anmerkungen aus dem Französischen des Herrn Abt Mably übersetzt*. Zurich, Switzerland: Heidegger.

Mann, H. (1844a). *Seventh Annual Report of the [Massachusetts] Board of Education, Together with the Seventh Annual Report of the Secretary of the Board*. Boston, MA: Dutton and Wentworth.

Mann, H. (1844b). *Reply to the "Remarks" of the Thirty-one Boston Schoolmasters on the Seventh Annual Report of the Secretary of the Massachusetts Board of Education*. Boston, MA: W.B. Fowle and N. Capen.

Mann, H. (1845). What God does, and what he leaves for man to do, in the work of education. In H. Mann (ed.), *Lectures on Education* (pp. 163–211). Boston, MA: Fowle and Capen.

Mansfield, E. D. (1851). *American Education, its Principles and Elements: Dedicated to the Teachers of the United States*. New York, NY: A. S. Barnes & Co.

Marti, J. R. (2009). Johann Rudolf Marti an Pestalozzi vom 23. September 1803. In R. Horlacher and D. Tröhler (eds), *Sämtliche Briefe an Pestalozzi, Volume I* (pp. 649–651). Zürich, Switzerland: NZZ Libro. (Written 1803)

Meyer, J. (1822). *Wie Herr Joseph Schmid die Pestalozzische Anstalt leitet*. Stuttgart, Germany: Metzler.

Meyer, J. (1823). *Aux amis de Pestalozzi: Réponse aux injures et fausses allégations*. Paris, France: David.

Monroe, P. (1908). *A Brief Course in the History of Education*. New York, NY: Macmillan Company.

Monroe, P. (1940). *Founding of the American Public School System: A History of Education in the United States; From the Early Settlements to the Close of the Civil War Period*. New York, NY: MacMillan.

Montesquieu, C.-L. (1748). *De l'esprit des loix, ou, du rapport que les loix doivent avoir avec la constitution de chaque gouvernement, les moeurs, le climat, la religion, le commerce, &c*. Geneva, Switzerland: chez Barillot, & fils.

Montesquieu, C.-L. (1750). *The Spirit of Laws. Translated from the French of M. de Secondat, Baron de Montesquieu. With Corrections and Additions Communicated by the Author*. London, UK: J. Nourse, and P. Vaillant, in the Strand.

Morf, H. (1885). *Zur Biographie Pestalozzis: Ein Beitrag zur Geschichte der Volkserziehung. Dritter Theil*. Winterthur, Switzerland: Bleuler-Hausheer & Cie.

Morf, H. (1889). *Zur Biographie Pestalozzi's: Ein Beitrag der Volksschule. Vierter Theil*. Winterthur, Germany: Geschwister Ziegler.

Moser, C. F. (1793). Was gibt es für Mittel, durch welche ein Schulmeister, der keine Profession erlernt hat, auch bei geringem

Einkommen sich doch bei Ehren halten kann? *Taschenbuch für teutsche Schulmeister, 8*, 237-249.

Müller, C. M. (1762). *Ansprache zur Eröffnung der Gesellschaft [Speech upon the Opening of the Society]*. Zurich, Switzerland: Zentralbibliothek. Ms Bodmer 37.3, Folder 2, f.0 8r-11v.

Munizipalität Payerne. (2009). Munizipalität Payerne an Pestalozzi vom 19. Juni 1804. In R. Horlacher and D. Tröhler (eds), *Sämtliche Briefe an Pestalozzi, Volume I* (pp. 710-711). Zürich, Switzerland: NZZ Libro. (Written 1804)

Munizipalität Yverdon. (2009). Munizipalität Yverdon an Pestalozzi vom 14. Februar 1804 In R. Horlacher and D. Tröhler (eds), *Sämtliche Briefe an Pestalozzi, Volume I* (pp. 688-690). Zurich, Switzerland: NZZ Libro. (Written 1804)

Neue Interimsrepublic. (1776). *Ephemeriden der Menschheit, 1*(1), 103-105.

Neueste Mode in der Pädagogik. (1803). *Journal des Luxus und der Moden, 18*, 195-202.

Nicolovius, G. H. L. (2009). Brief an Pestalozzi 14. November 1792 [Letter to Pestalozzi 14 November 1792]. In R. Horlacher and D. Tröhler (eds), *Sämtliche Briefe an Pestalozzi, Volume 1* (pp. 266-268). Zurich, Switzerland: NZZ Libro. (Written 1792)

Nicolovius, G. H. L. (2009). Brief an Pestalozzi 14. November 1794 [Letter to Pestalozzi 14 November 1794]. In R. Horlacher and D. Tröhler (eds), *Sämtliche Briefe an Pestalozzi, Volume 1* (pp. 279-282). Zurich, Switzerland: NZZ Libro. (Written 1794)

Nicolovius, G. H. L. (2010). Nicolovius an Pestalozzi vom 19. September 1808. In R. Horlacher and D. Tröhler (eds), *Sämtliche Briefe an Pestalozzi, Volume II* (pp. 552-553). Zurich, Switzerland: NZZ Libro. (Written 1808)

Niederer, J. (1811). *Das Pestalozzische Institut an das Publikum - eine Schutzrede gegen verläumderische Angriffe*. Yverdon, Switzerland.

Niederer, J. (1829). Der pädagogische Geistessumpf unserer Zeit und das Quaken darin gegen die Pestalozzi'sche Schule. Erstes Beispiel. Herr Dr. Diesterweg in Mörs. *J. P. Rossel's allgemeine Monatschrift für Erziehung und Unterricht, 6*, 174-187.

Niederer, J. (2010). Brief an Pestalozzi vom 20. September 1808. In R. Horlacher and D. Tröhler (eds), *Sämtliche Briefe an Pestalozzi, Volume 2* (pp. 553-558). Zurich, Switzerland: NZZ Libro. (Written 1808)

Niederer, J., Krüsi, H., and Naef, J. K. (1827). Erklärung zu Pestalozzis Tode. *Rheinisch-westfälische Monatschrift für Erziehung und Volksunterricht, 4*, 67-72.

Nugent, T. (1749). *The Grand Tour – Containing an Exact Description of Most of the Cities, Towns and Remarkable Places of Europe*. London, UK: Printed for S. Birt, D. Browne, A. Millar, and G. Hawkins.

Painter, F. V N. (1886). *A History of Education*. New York, NY: D. Appleton.

Parsons, T. (1971). *The System of Modern Societies*. Englewood Cliffs, NJ: Prentice-Hall.

Pensylvanische Regierungsform. (1777). *Ephemeriden der Menschheit*, 2(4), 76–78.

Pestalozzi, J. H. (1951). Brief an Johann Baptist von Tscharner vom 20. Mai 1804 [Letter to Johann Baptist von Tscharner 20 May 1804]. In E. Dejung and H. Stettbacher (eds), *Johann Heinrich Pestalozzi, Sämtliche Briefe, Volume 4* (pp. 199–200). Zurich, Switzerland: Orell Füssli. (Written 1804)

Pestalozzi, J. H. (1781). *Lienhard und Gertrud: ein Buch für das Volk*. Berlin, Germany: George Decker.

Pestalozzi, J. H. (1783). *Léonard et Gertrude ou les moeurs villageoises, telles qu´on les retrouve à la Ville et à la Cour*. Lausanne, Switzerland: chez Gabriel Decombaz (Translation of Pestalozzi, 1781)

Pestalozzi, J. H. (1783). *Ueber Gesetzgebung und Kindermord, Wahrheiten und Träume, Nachforschungen und Bilder: Vom Verfasser Lienhardts und Gertrud* [On Laws and Infanticide, Truths and Dreams, Inquiries and Pictures: From the Author of Leonard & Gertrude]. Frankfurt and Leipzig, Germany: Auf Kosten des Verfassers, und in Kommißion bey der Buchhandlung der Gelehrten.

Pestalozzi, J. H. (1800). *Leonard & Gertrude: A Popular Story, Written Originally in German; Translated into French, and Now Attempted in English; with the Hope of Its Being Useful to the Lower Orders of Society*. Bath, UK: Printed and sold by S. Hazard. (Translation of Pestalozzi, 1783/1781)

Pestalozzi, J. H. (1801). *Leonard & Gertrude: A Popular Story, Written Originally in German; Translated into French, and Now Attempted in English; with the Hope of Its Being Useful to the Lower Orders of Society*. Philadelphia, PA: J. Groff.

Pestalozzi, J. H. (1803a). *Anschauungslehre der Zahlenverhältnisse*. Zurich, Switzerland: Gessner.

Pestalozzi, J. H. (1803b). *Buch der Mütter oder Anleitung für Mütter ihre Kinder bemerken und reden zu lehren*. Zurich, Switzerland: Gessner.

Pestalozzi, J. H. (1803/1804). *Anschauungslehre der Zahlenverhältnisse*. Zurich, Switzerland: Gessner.

Pestalozzi, J. H. (1826a). *Meine Lebensschicksale als Vorsteher meiner Erziehungsinstitute in Burgdorf und Iferten* [My Life's Destiny as Head of My Education Institutes in Burgdorf and Iferten]. Leipzig, Germany: Fleischer.

Pestalozzi, J. H. (1826b). *Pestalozzi's sämmtliche Schriften: Volume 13 Schwanengesang* [Swan song]. Stuttgart, Germany: Cotta.

Pestalozzi, J. H. (1894). *How Gertrude Teaches Her Children: An Attempt to Help Mothers to Teach their Own Children and an Account of the Method*. London, UK: Swan Sonnenschein. Available at: http://archive.org/stream/howgertrudeteachoopestuoft/howgertrudeteachoopestuoft_djvu.txt

Pestalozzi, J. H. (1927a). Scenen im Innern Frankreichs, nach der Natur gezeichnet. In A. Buchenau, E. Spranger and H. Stettbacher (eds), *Pestalozzis Sämtliche Werke, Volume 8* (pp. 23-30). (First published 1782)

Pestalozzi, J. H. (1927b). Über den Bauern. In A. Buchenau, E. Spranger and H. Stettbacher (eds), *Pestalozzis Sämtliche Werke, Volume 8* (pp. 47-56). (First published 1782)

Pestalozzi, J. H. (1927c). Wieder vom Bauern. In A. Buchenau, E. Spranger and H. Stettbacher (eds), *Pestalozzis Sämtliche Werke, Volume 8* (pp. 57-64). (First published 1782)

Pestalozzi, J. H. (1928). Lienhard und Gertrud. Ein Buch für's Volk. Dritter Theil. In A. Buchenau, E. Spranger and H. Stettbacher (eds), *Pestalozzis Sämtliche Werke, Volume 3* (pp. 1-236). Berlin, Germany: Walter de Gruyter. (First published 1785)

Pestalozzi, J. H. (1928). Lienhard und Gertrude: Ein Buch für's Volk. Vierter und letzter Theil. In A. Buchenau, E. Spranger and H. Stettbacher (eds), *Pestalozzis Sämtliche Werke, Volume 4* (pp. 237-504). Berlin, Germany: Walter de Gruyter. (First published 1787)

Pestalozzi, J. H. (1930). Fragment über den Stand der Natur und der Gesellschaft [Fragment on the state of nature and society]. In A. Buchenau, E. Spranger and H. Stettbacher (eds), *Pestalozzis Sämtliche Werke, Volume 9* (pp. 205-238). Berlin, Germany: Walter de Gruyter. (Written 1783)

Pestalozzi, J. H. (1931a). Ja oder Nein? Aüsserungen über die bürgerliche Stimmung der europäischen Menschheit in den oberen und unteren Stenden, von einem freyen Man. In A. Buchenau, E. Spranger and H. Stettbacher (eds), *Pestalozzis Sämtliche Werke, Volume 10* (pp. 75-170). Berlin, Germany: Walter de Gruyter. (Written 1793)

Pestalozzi, J. H. (1931b). Über Sansculottismus undn Christentum. In A. Buchenau, E. Spranger and H. Stettbacher (eds), *Pestalozzis Sämtliche Werke, Volume 10* (pp. 263-268). Berlin, Germany: Walter de Gruyter. (Written 1794)

Pestalozzi, J. H. (1931c). An die Freunde der Freiheit am Zürichsee und der Enden. In A. Buchenau, E. Spranger and H. Stettbacher (eds), *Pestalozzis Sämtliche Werke, Volume 10* (pp. 303-311). Berlin, Germany: Walter de Gruyter. (Written 1795)

Pestalozzi, J. H. (1932). Agis. In A. Buchenau, E. Spranger and H. Stettbacher (eds), *Pestalozzis Sämtliche Werke, Volume 1* (pp. 1-21). Berlin, Germany: Walter de Gruyter. (First published 1765)

Pestalozzi, J. H. (1932). Herrn Pestalotz Briefe and Herrn N. E. T. über die Erziehung der armen Landjungen [Mr. Pestalozzi's letters and Mr. N. E. T. on the education of poor country youth]. In A. Buchenau, E. Spranger and H. Stettbacher (eds), *Pestalozzis Sämtliche Werke, Volume 1* (pp. 142-175). Berlin, Germany: Walter de Gruyter. (Written 1777)

Pestalozzi, J. H. (1932). Pestalozzis Brief an einen Freund über seinen Aufenthalt in Stanz [Pestalozzi's letter to a friend about his stay in Stans]. In A. Buchenau, E. Spranger and H. Stettbacher (eds), *Pestalozzis Sämtliche Werke, Volume 13* (pp. 1-32). Berlin, Germany: Walter de Gruyter. (Written 1807)

Pestalozzi, J. H. (1932). Von der Freyheit meiner Vaterstatt! [On the freedom of my father city!]. In A. Buchenau, E. Spranger and H. Stettbacher (eds), *Pestalozzis Sämtliche Werke, Volume 1* (pp. 203-244). Berlin, Germany: Walter de Gruyter. (Written 1779)

Pestalozzi, J. H. (1932). Wie Gertrud ihre Kinder lehrt, ein Versuch, den Müttern Anleitung zu geben, ihre Kinder selbst zu unterrichten, in Briefen. In A. Buchenau, E. Spranger and H. Stettbacher (eds), *Pestalozzis Sämtliche Werke, Volume 13* (pp. 181-359). Berlin, Germany: Walter de Gruyter. (First published 1801)

Pestalozzi. J. H. (1935). Abschiedsworte an die Kinder in Münchenbuchsee. In W. Feilchenfeld-Fales and H. Schönebaum (eds), *Pestalozzi Sämtliche Werke, Volume 16* (pp. 225-228). Berlin, Germany: Walter de Gruyter. (Written 1804)

Pestalozzi, J. H. (1938). Meine Nachforschungen über den Gang der Natur in der Entwicklung des Menschengeschlechts. In A. Buchenau,

E. Spranger and H. Stettbacher (eds), *Pestalozzis Sämtliche Werke*, Volume 12 (pp. 1–166). (First published 1797)

Pestalozzi, J. H. (1938). Zuruf an die vormals demokratischen Kantone. In A. Buchenau, E. Spranger, and H. Stettbacher (eds), *Pestalozzis Sämtliche Werke*, Volume 12 (pp. 275–282). Berlin, Germany: Walter de Gruyter. (Written 1798)

Pestalozzi, J. H. (1943a). Zweck und Plan einer Armenanstalt. In A. Buchenau, E. Spranger and H. Stettbacher (eds), *Pestalozzis Sämtliche Werke*, Volume 18 (pp. 53–76). Berlin, Germany: Walter de Gruyter. (Written 1805)

Pestalozzi, J. H. (1943b). Aufruf für die Armenanstalt. In A. Buchenau, E. Spranger and H. Stettbacher (eds), *Pestalozzis Sämtliche Werke*, Volume 18 (pp. 77–80). Berlin, Germany: Walter de Gruyter. (Written 1805)

Pestalozzi, J. H. (1943c). Über Volksbildung und Industrie. In A. Buchenau, E. Spranger and H. Stettbacher (eds), *Pestalozzis Sämtliche Werke*, Volume 18 (pp. 139–169). Berlin, Germany: Walter de Gruyter. (Written 1806)

Pestalozzi, J. H. (1943d). Ein Gespräch über Volksaufklärung und Volksbildung. In A. Buchenau, E. Spranger and H. Stettbacher (eds), *Pestalozzis Sämtliche Werke*, Volume 18 (pp. 175–193). Berlin, Germany: Walter de Gruyter. (Written 1806)

Pestalozzi, J. H. (1946). Brief an Anna Schulthess Anfang Juli 1767 [Letter to Anna Schulthess, beginning of July 1767]. In E. Dejung and H. Stettbacher (eds), *Johann Heinrich Pestalozzi, Sämtliche Briefe*, Volume 1 (pp. 25–35). Zurich, Switzerland: Orell Füssli. (Written 1767)

Pestalozzi, J. H. (1946). Brief an Anna Schulthess 4. Oktober 1767 [Letter to Anna Schulthess, 4 October 1767]. In E. Dejung and H. Stettbacher (eds), *Johann Heinrich Pestalozzi, Sämtliche Briefe*, Volume 1 (pp. 121–125). Zurich, Switzerland: Orell Füssli. (Written 1767)

Pestalozzi, J. H. (1949). Brief an Karl Johann Christian von Zinzendorf 26. Mai 1787 [Letter to Karl Johann Christian von Zinzendorf, 26 May 1787]. In E. Dejung and H. Stettbacher (eds), *Johann Heinrich Pestalozzi, Sämtliche Briefe*, Volume 3 (pp. 244–246). Zurich, Switzerland: Orell Füssli. (Written 1787)

Pestalozzi, J. H. (1949). Brief an Georg Heinrich Ludwig Nicolovius 1. Oktober 1793 [Letter to Georg Heinrich Ludwig Nicolovius 1 October 1793]. In E. Dejung and H. Stettbacher (eds), *Johann*

Heinrich Pestalozzi, Sämtliche Briefe, Volume 3 (pp. 298-302). Zurich, Switzerland: Orell Füssli. (Written 1793)

Pestalozzi, J. H. (1949). Brief an Philipp Emanuel von Fellenberg 15. November 1793 [Letter to Philipp Emanuel von Fellenberg, 16 November 1793]. In E. Dejung and H. Stettbacher (eds), *Johann Heinrich Pestalozzi, Sämtliche Briefe, Volume 3* (pp. 303-306). Zurich, Switzerland: Orell Füssli. (Written 1793)

Pestalozzi, J. H. (1951). Letter sent to the minister of Justice Meyer, May 1798. In E. Dejung and H. Stettbacher (eds), *Johann Heinrich Pestalozzi, Sämtliche Briefe, Volume 4* (p. 15). Zurich, Switzerland: Orell Füssli. (Written 1798)

Pestalozzi, J. H. (1952). Bemerkungen zum Matthäusevangelium. In E. Dejung, W. Feilchenfeld Fales, W. Klauser, A. Rufer and H. Schönebaum (eds), *Pestalozzis Sämtliche Werke, Volume XIV* (pp. 33-49). Berlin, Germany: de Gruyter. (First published 1802)

Pestalozzi, J. H. (1961a). Pestalozzi an David Vogel vom Anfang September 1805. In E. Dejung and W. Feilchenfeld Fales (eds), *Pestalozzis Sämtliche Briefe, Volume V* (pp. 35-36). Zurich, Switzerland: Orell Füssli. (Written 1805)

Pestalozzi, J. H. (1961b). Pestalozzi an Johannes Niederer vom 20. September 1805 (1805/1961). In E. Dejung and W. Feilchenfeld Fales (eds), *Pestalozzis Sämtliche Briefe, Volume V* (p. 43). Zurich, Switzerland: Orell Füssli. (Written 1805)

Pestalozzi, J. H. (1961c). Pestalozzi an Paul Usteri vom Mai 1807. In E. Dejung and W. Feilchenfeld Fales (eds), *Pestalozzis Sämtliche Briefe, Volume V* (pp. 251-255). Zurich, Switzerland: Orell Füssli. (Written 1807)

Pestalozzi, J. H. (1964a). Am Neujahrstage 1808. In A. Buchenau, E. Spranger and H. Stettbacher (eds), *Pestalozzis Sämtliche Werke, Volume 21* (pp. 1-9). Zurich, Switzerland: Orell Füssli. (Written 1808)

Pestalozzi, J. H. (1964b). Rede über die Aufsicht. In A. Buchenau, E. Spranger and H. Stettbacher (eds), *Pestalozzis Sämtliche Werke, Volume 21* (pp. 205-212). Zurich, Switzerland: Orell Füssli. (Written 1808)

Pestalozzi, J. H. (1964c). Zuschrift an die Versammlung der Stellvertreter aller Kantone der Schweizerischen Eidgenossenschaft, gerichtet an Landamman d'Affry. In A. Buchenau, E. Spranger and H. Stettbacher (eds), *Pestalozzis Sämtliche Werke, Volume 21* (pp. 271-276). (Written 1809)

Pestalozzi, J. H. (1964d). Eingabe an Landamman d'Affry in Freiburg. 9. August 1809. Mit zwei Beilagen. In A. Buchenau, E. Spranger and H. Stettbacher (eds), *Pestalozzis Sämtliche Werke, Volume 21* (pp. 277-292). (Written 1809)

Pestalozzi, J. H. (1969). Brief an Nicolovius 8. Dezember 1819 [Letter to Nicolovius 8 December 1819]. In E. Dejung and H. Stettbacher (eds), *Johann Heinrich Pestalozzi, Sämtliche Briefe, Volume 11* (pp. 309-312). Zurich, Switzerland: Orell Füssli. (Written 1819)

Pestalozzi, J. H. (1971a). Brief an den Staatsrat des Kantons Waadt 16. Oktober 1824 [Letter to the state council of the Canton of Vaud 16 October 1824]. In E. Dejung and H. Stettbacher (eds), *Johann Heinrich Pestalozzi, Sämtliche Briefe, Volume 13* (pp. 178-183). Zurich, Switzerland: Orell Füssli. (Written 1824)

Pestalozzi, J. H. (1971b). Brief an den Stadtrat Yverdon 3. November 1824 [Letter to the city council of Yverdon 3 November 1824]. In E. Dejung and H. Stettbacher (eds), *Johann Heinrich Pestalozzi, Sämtliche Briefe, Volume 13* (pp. 187-189). Zurich, Switzerland: Orell Füssli. (Written 1824)

Pestalozzi, J. H. (1971c). Brief an den Stadtrat Yverdon 9. November 1824 [Letter to the city council of Yverdon 9 November 1824]. In E. Dejung and H. Stettbacher (eds), *Johann Heinrich Pestalozzi, Sämtliche Briefe, Volume 13* (pp. 189-191). Zurich, Switzerland: Orell Füssli. (Written 1824)

Pestalozzi, J. H. (1971d). Brief an Joseph Schmid 27. Juni 1825 [Letter to Joseph Schmid 27 June 1825]. In E. Dejung and H. Stettbacher (eds), *Johann Heinrich Pestalozzi, Sämtliche Briefe, Volume 13* (pp. 273-279). Zurich, Switzerland: Orell Füssli. (Written 1825)

Pestalozzi, J. H. (1976a). Entgegnung auf Eduard Bibers Buch: Beitrag zur Biographie Heinrich Pestalozzis, St. Gallen 1827. In A. Buchenau, E. Spranger and H. Stettbacher (eds), *Pestalozzis Sämtliche Werke, Volume 28* (pp. 349-373). (Written 1827)

Pestalozzi, J. H. (1976b). Grabschrift. In A. Buchenau, E. Spranger and H. Stettbacher (eds), *Pestalozzis Sämtliche Werke, Volume 28* (p. 380). (Written 1827)

Pestalozzi, J. H. (1976c). Letzte Willenserklärung. In A. Buchenau, E. Spranger and H. Stettbacher (eds), *Pestalozzis Sämtliche Werke, Volume 28* (pp. 377-379). (Written 1827)

Pestalozzi, J. H. (1977). An die Unschuld, den Ernst und den Edelmut meines Zeitalters und meines Vaterlandes. Ein Wort zur Zeit. In

A. Buchenau, E. Spranger and H. Stettbacher (eds), *Pestalozzis Sämtliche Werke*, Volume 24A (pp. 1-222). (First published 1815)

Pestalozzi, J. H. (1998). Brief an Friedrich Heinrich Jacobi 22. April 1794 [Letter to Friedrich Heinrich Jacobi 22 April 1794]. In Daniel Tröhler (ed.), *Pestalozzis 'Nachforschungen' I: textimmanente Studien. 18 neuentdeckte Briefe Pestalozzis* (pp. 184-190). Bern, Switzerland: Haupt. (Written 1794).

Peyer, H. C. (1968). *Von Handel und Bank im alten Zürich* [On trade and banks in old Zurich]. Zurich, Switzerland: Berichthaus.

Phelps, W. F. (1857). Normal schools, their relations to primary and higher institutions of learning, and to the progress of society. *American Journal of Education*, 3, 417-427.

Plamann, J. E. (1805a). *Anordnung des Unterrichts für die Pestalozzische Knabenschule in Berlin*. Berlin, Germany: Hayn.

Plamann, J. E. (1805b). *Einzige Grundregel der Unterrichtskunst nach Pestalozzis Methode angewandt in der Naturgeschichte, Geographie und Sprache*. Halle, Germany: Renger.

Plamann, J. E. (1806). *Elementarformen des Sprach- und wissenschaftlichen Unterrichts nach Pestalozzi's Grundsätzen. Theil 1, Bd. 3: Naturbeschreibung*. Berlin, Germany: Sander.

Plamann, J. E. (1812/1815). *Beiträge zur Vertheidigung der Pestalozzischen Methode, Volumes I+II*. Leipzig, Germany: Rein.

Plato. (1966). *The Republic*. Cambridge, UK: Cambridge University Press.

Plum, F. (1803). *Pestalozzis Læremaade. Et Forsøg til Elementar-Underviisningens Forbedring: Med indbydels til en Oversættelse af Pestalozzi's Elementarbøger*. Copenhagen, Denmark: Morthorstes Enke.

Pocock, J G. A. (1975). *The Machiavellian Moment: Florentine Political Thought and the Atlantic Republican Tradition*. Princeton, NJ: Princeton University Press.

Pocock, J. G. A. (1985). The mobility of property and the rise of eighteenth-century sociology. In J. G. A. Pocock, *Virtue, Commerce, and History* (pp. 103-123). Cambridge, UK: Cambridge University Press.

Popkewitz, T. S. (1984). *Paradigm and Ideology in Educational Research: the Social Functions of the Intellectual*. London, UK: Falmer Press.

Raab, F. (1964): *The English Face of Machiavelli: A Changing Interpretation, 1500-1700*. London, UK: Routledge.

Raumer, K. von. (1857). The life and educational system of Pestalozzi. *American Journal of Education*, 3, 401-416.

Riemann, K. F. (1804) Von Rochow und Pestalozzi; Oder: Über die Basis des Volksunterrichts. *Neue Berlinische Monatsschrift*, 1, 123–137.

Rousseau J.-J. (1755). *Discours sur l'origine et les fondemens de l'inégalité parmi les hommes / par Jean-Jacques Rousseau*. Amsterdam, The Netherlands: M.-M. Rey.

Rousseau, J.-J. (1979). *Emile or on Education* (A. Bloom, trans., ed.). New York, NY: Basic Books. (Original work published 1762)

Rousseau, J.-J. (2002). The social contract. In S. Dunn (ed.), *Jean-Jacques Rousseau, The Social Contract and the First and Second Discourses* (pp. 149–254). New Haven, CT: Yale University Press. (Original work published 1762)

Sauer, M. (1987). *Volksschullehrerbildung in Preußen: Die Seminare und Präparandenanstalten vom 18. Jahrhundert bis zur Weimarer Republik*. Cologne, Germany: Böhlau Verlag.

Schiller, F. von (1804). *Wilhelm Tell*. Tübingen, Germany: J. G. Cotta.

Schmid, J. (1809/1811). *Die Elemente der Form und Grösse (gewöhnlich Geometrie genannt), nach Pestalozzis Grundsätzen bearbeitet, Volumes 1–3*. Bern, Switzerland: Wittwe Stämpfli (Volume 1), Ludwig Albrecht Haller (Volume 2), Heidelberg, Germany: Mohr, Zimmer.

Schmid, J. (1822). *Wahrheit und Irrtum in Pestalozzis Lebensschicksalen*. Yverdon, Switzerland.

Scholz, J. (2011). Die *Lehrer leuchten wie die Sterne. Landschulreform und Elementarlehrerbildung in Brandenburg-Preußen*. Bremen, Germany: Edition Lumière.

Schrötter, F. L. von. (2010). Schrötter an Pestalozzi vom 11. September 1808. In R. Horlacher and D. Tröhler (eds), *Sämtliche Briefe an Pestalozzi, Volume II* (pp. 540–543). Zurich, Switzerland: NZZ Libro. (Written 1808)

Schulthess, A. (1993). [Diary]. In F.-P. Hager and D. Tröhler (eds), *Anna Pestalozzis Tagebuch. Käte Silber: Anna Pestalozzi und der Frauenkreis um Pestalozzi* (pp. 5–72). Bern, Switzerland: Haupt. (Written 1798)

Schulthess, A. (1946). Brief an Pestalozzi vom 24. September 1767 [Letter to Pestalozzi, 24 September 1767]. In E. Dejung and H. Stettbacher (eds), *Johann Heinrich Pestalozzi, Sämtliche Briefe, Volume 1* (pp. 113–120). Zurich, Switzerland: Orell Füssli. (Written 1767)

Seeley, L. (1899). *History of Education*. New York, NY: American Book Company.

Shoup, W. J. (1891). *The History and Science of Education: for Institutes, Normal Schools, Reading Circles and the Private Self-Instruction of Teachers*. New York, NY: American Book Company.

Sektion Unterricht des preussischen Innenministerium. (2010a). Sektion Unterricht des preussischen Innenministerium an Pestalozzi vom 10. Mai 1809. In R. Horlacher and D. Tröhler (eds), *Sämtliche Briefe an Pestalozzi, Volume II* (pp. 691–692). Zurich, Switzerland: Nzz Libro. (Written 1809)

Sektion Unterricht des preussischen Innenministerium. (2010b). Sektion Unterricht des preussischen Innenministerium an Pestalozzi vom 15. August 1809. In R. Horlacher and D. Tröhler (eds), *Sämtliche Briefe an Pestalozzi, Volume 2* (pp. 744–746). Zurich, Switzerland: NZZ Libro. (Written 1809)

Skinner, Q. (1988): Meaning and understanding in the history of ideas. In James Tully (ed.), *Meaning and Context: Quentin Skinner and His Critics* (pp. 29–67). Princeton, NJ: Princeton University Press.

Skinner, Q. (2002a). Meaning and understanding in the history of ideas. In Q. Skinner, *Visions of Politics: Vol. I. Regarding Method* (pp. 57–89). Cambridge, UK: Cambridge University Press.

Skinner, Q. (2002b). The practice of history and the cult of the fact. In Q. Skinner, *Visions of Politics: Vol. I. Regarding Method* (pp. 8–26). Cambridge, UK: Cambridge University Press.

Skipwith, F., and Maclure, W. (2010). Skipwith und Maclure an Pestalozzi vom Juli 1807. In R. Horlacher and D. Tröhler (eds), *Sämtliche Briefe an Pestalozzi, Volume II* (pp. 261–263). Zurich, Switzerland: NZZ Libro. (Written 1807)

Skrabec, Q. R. (2009). *William McGuffey: Mentor to American Industry*. New York, NY: Algora Publishing.

Smith, T. L. (1957). *Revivalism & Social Reform: American Protestantism on the Eve of the Civil War*. Baltimore, MD: The Johns Hopkins University Press.

Soëtard, M. (1981). *Pestalozzi ou la naissance de l'éducateur: Étude sur l'évolution de la pensée et de l'action du pédagogue suisse (1746–1827)*. Bern, Switzerland: Peter Lang.

Soyaux, A. W. F. (1803). *Pestalozzi, seine Lehrart und seine Anstalt*. Leipzig, Germany: bei Gerhard Fleischer d. Jüngeren.

Statutes. (1762). Zurich, Switzerland: Zentralbibliothek Zürich, Ms Bodmer 37.4, Folder 1, f.o 1r–6v.

Steinmüller, J. R. (1803). *Bemerkungen gegen Pestalozzis Unterrichtsmethode – nebst einigen Beylagen, das Landschulwesen betreffend.* Zurich, Switzerland: Orell Füssli.

Stourzh, G. (1970). *Alexander Hamilton and the Idea of American Government.* Stanford, CA: Stanford University Press.

Südpreussisches Departement. (2009). Südpreussisches Departement an Pestalozzi vom 19. Juli 1803. In R. Horlacher and D. Tröhler (eds), *Sämtliche Briefe an Pestalozzi, Band I* (pp. 620-621). Zurich, Switzerland: NZZ Libro. (Written 1803)

Trenchard, J, & Gordon, T. (1995). *Cato's Letters Or Essays on Liberty, Civil and Religious, and Other Important Subjects* (R. Hamowy, ed.). Indianapolis, IN: Liberty Fund. (First published 1720-1723)

Tröhler, D. (2006). The "Kingdom of God on Earth" and early Chicago pragmatism. *Educational Theory,* 56(1), 89-105.

Tröhler, D. (2009). Curriculum, languages, and mentalities. In B. Baker (ed.), *New Curriculum History* (pp. 97-115). Rotterdam, The Netherlands: Sense Publishers.

Tröhler, D. (2010). Harmonizing the educational globe: world polity, cultural features, and the challenges to educational research. In *Studies in Philosophy and Education,* 29, 7-29.

Tröhler D. (2010a). The technological sublime and social diversity: Chicago pragmatism as response to a cultural construction of modernity. In D. Tröhler, T. Schlag and F. Osterwalder (eds), *Pragmatism and Modernities.* Rotterdam, The Netherlands: Sense Publishers.

Tröhler, D. (2011a). *Languages of Education: Protestant Legacies, National Identities, and Global Aspirations.* New York, NY: Routledge.

Tröhler, D. (2011b). The educationalization of the modern world. Progress, passion, and the Protestant promise of education. In D. Tröhler, *Languages of Education: Protestant Legacies, National Identities, and Global Aspirations* (pp. 21-36). New York, NY: Routledge.

Tröhler, D. (in press). Change management in the governance of schooling: the rise of experts, planners, and statistics in the early OECD. *Teachers College Record, 115.*

Tröhler, D., Popkewitz, T. S., and Labaree, D. F. (2011): Children, citizens, and promised lands: comparative history of political cultures and schooling in the long 19th century. In D. Tröhler, T. S. Popkewitz and D. F. David F. Labaree (Eds.), *Schooling and the Making of Citizens in the Long Nineteenth Century: Comparative Visions* (pp. 1-27). New York, NY: Routledge.

Tscharner, N. E. (1776/77): Briefe über die Armenanstalten auf dem Land [Letters on the poorhouses in the countryside]. *Ephemeriden der Menschheit*, 1. Stück [1776], 43–48 (= 1. Brief); 5. Stück [1776], 15–25 (= 2. Brief); 6. Stück [1776], 53–79 (= 3.–7. Brief); 11. Stück [1776], 18–51 (= 8.–12. Brief); 3. Stück [1777], 1–36 (= 13.–17. Brief).

Tscharner, J. B. von. (2009). Tscharner an Pestalozzi vom Mai 1804. In R. Horlacher and D. Tröhler (eds), *Sämtliche Briefe an Pestalozzi, Volume I* (p. 707). Zurich, Switzerland: NZZ Libro. (Written 1804)

Türk, W. C. von. (2010). Wilhelm Christian von Türk an Pestalozzi vom 25. Januar 1805. In R. Horlacher and D. Tröhler (eds), *Sämtliche Briefe an Pestalozzi, Volume 2* (p. 13–22). Zurich, Switzerland: NZZ Libro. (Written 1805)

Unger, H. G. (2009). *The Last Founding Father: James Monroe and a Nation's Call to Greatness*. Cambridge, MA: Da Capo Press.

Volz-Tobler, B. (1997). *Rebellion im Namen der Tugend. 'Der Erinnerer' – eine Moralische Wochenschrift, Zürich 1765-1767* [*Rebellion in the Name of Virtue: 'the Reminder' a Moral Weekly*]. Zurich, Switzerland: Chronos.

Wehrli, M. (ed.) (1989). *Das geistige Zürich im 18. Jahrhundert: Texte und Dokumente von Gotthard Heidegger bis Heinrich Pestalozzi* [*Intellectual Zurich in the Eighteenth Century: Texts and Documents from Gotthard Heidegger to Heinrich Pestalozzi*]. Basel, Switzerland: Birkhäuser.

Weiss, C. (1803). Über die Nothwendigkeit, die Erziehungskunst wissenschaftlich zu behandeln. *Beiträge zur Erziehungskunst, zur Vervollkommnung sowohl ihrer Grundsätze als ihrer Methode*, 1, 1–26.

Willcox, W. B. (ed.) (1987). *The Papers of Benjamin Franklin, Volume 26*. New Haven, CT: Yale University Press.

Wolfowitz, P. (2007). Foreword. In World Bank, *World Development Report 2007: Development and the Next Generation* (p. xi). Washington, DC: The International Bank for Reconstruction and Development / The World Bank.

Wood, G. S. (1969). *The Creation of the American Republic 1776–1787*. Chapel Hill, NC: University of North Carolina Press.

Wysling, H. (ed.) (1983). *Zürich im 18. Jahrhundert* [*Zurich in the Eighteenth Century*]. Zurich, Switzerland: Berichthaus.

Zehnder-Stadlin, J. (1875). *Pestalozzi: Idee und Macht der menschlichen Entwicklung* [*Pestalozzi: Idea and Power of Human Development*]. Gotha, Germany: Thienemann.

Ziemssen, T. (1804). *Dissertatio paedagogica de Pestalozziana institutionis methodo. Particula prima, sistens generaliora hujus methodi principa.* Doctoral dissertation. Greifswald, Germany: Eckhardt.

Index

activists, 87–90
Act of Mediation, 84
Adams, John, 16
Addresses to the German Nation (Fichte), 80, 100–3
agrarian life, 31, 33–4
alienation, 40
Allen, William, 132–3
American Journal of Education, 126–7
American Revolution, 4
Ancien Régime, 3
An die Unschuld, den Ernst und den Edelmut (Pestalozzi), 111–13
Anglican Church, 15
aristocracy, 15–16, 51, 53

Bank Leu, 18
Bank of England, 6, 11n4, 18
banks, 18–19, 24n6
Barnard, Henry, 126, 137
Batavian Republic, 63
Belgium, 3, 124
Berliner Monatsschrift, 44
Biber, Eduard, 121–2, 127n2
Biester, Johann Erich, 44, 79
Bodmer, Johann Jacob, 20–1, 23, 28
Bonaparte, Louis Napoleon, 87
Bonaparte, Napoleon, 63
 see also Napoleon I
Bonnot de Mably, Gabriel, 9, 13n13, 28

Breitinger, Johann Jacob, 20

Calvin, Jean, 23n1
Calvinism, 9
Campe, Joachim Heinrich, 54, 60n2
capital
 export of, 18
 politics and, 6–8, 12n9
capitalism, 11n4
Catholic Church, 18, 23n1
Catholicism, 8–9
charisma, 95–104, 108
Charles IV, 86–7
Charter of 1830, 124
Christian ethics, 141
Christian republic, 39–42
Christian VII, 85–6
Cispadane Republic, 63
citizenship, 15–16, 24n4
city society, 19–21
civic virtue, 10
cognitive development, 70–1
Cold War, 140
commercial economy, 6–7, 12n10
commercialization, 17–19
commercial progress, 7–8
compulsory schooling, 3, 124
Condorcet, Marquis de, 5–6
Confederation of the Rhine, 87, 92n4
conflicts, 98–100, 121

Index

Congress of Vienna, 4, 63, 111, 118, 123, 130
constitutions, 8, 15, 17, 39, 51, 52, 124, 130
Continental System, 115, 132
corruption, 19–21
Cotta, 113
Cousin, Victor, 125–6

Davidson, Thomas, 138
Declaration of Independence, 16, 52, 63
Declaration of Rights of Man and Citizen, 63
Denmark, 3, 80, 85–6, 116n8
Dewey, John, 13n12 136
Diesterweg, Adolph, 124–5, 127n7

early industry, 9, 33–4, 40
economic crisis, 113–14
economic patriots, 34–6, 44
education
  compulsory, 3
  demands for new, 83–94
  "method," 63, 68–71, 74–6, 80–2, 85–93, 96, 98–100, 101–4, 106–9, 124
  modern, 2
  public, 3
  reform, 88–9, 130–2
  of rural poor, 35–6
  teacher, 2–3, 88, 136–9
  vocational, 45–6
educational methods, interest in, 83–94
educational public, 90–2
educational system, 73–82
educational turn, 1–13, 15, 48, 68, 89, 93n10, 125–6, 136–7
  Pestalozzi and, 2–4
  prehistory of, 4–6
  Protestantism and, 8–11
  Zurich, 14–25
education policy, 103–4
egoism, 45–6, 48, 53, 59–60
Emile (Rousseau), 2, 27, 30–1, 81

England, 5–8, 11n5, 12n10, 15, 35, 132
English Civil Wars, 11n5
English Pestalozzians, 132–3
Enlightenment, 44–7, 139–40
Era of Good Feelings, 132
Europe
  see also specific countries
  educational demands in, 83–94
Ewald, Johann Ludwig, 79

Fellenberg, Daniel von, 44,
Fellenberg, Philippe Emanuel von, 58, 106
Fichte, Johann Gottlieb, 20, 55–6, 58, 80, 100–4, 108, 142n1
Fischer, Johann Rudolf, 69
France, 3, 5, 8, 18, 35, 51–2, 56–7, 101, 104, 123–5, 137
Franco-Prussian War, 137
Franklin, Benjamin, 51–2
freedom
  economic, 15, 39–40, 57–8
  inward, 13n12, 56,
  political, 13n12, 15, 20–1, 23, 29, 40, 45, 48, 51–4, 56, 58–9, 61n3, 64, 72n6
French Revolution, 4–6, 47, 54–6, 61n3, 63–4, 72n8, 72n9, 130
Friedrich I, 87
Fröbel, Friedrich Wilhelm August, 91, 93n13
Füssli, Johann Heinrich [Fusely, Henry], 22–3, 25n21

German idealism, 51, 56, 72n9, 109
German nationalism, 101
German Protestantism, 9
German Romanticism, 72n9
Germany, 20, 23n1, 35, 49n7, 60n1, 60n2, 72n9, 76, 84, 86, 89, 91, 93n11, 93n13, 101–2, 108, 116n8, 121, 124–6, 136–7, 140, 143n6
Gessner, Salomon, 20
Goldmann, Lucien, 135
Gottsched, Johann Christoph, 20
Great Britain, 6, 12n6, 85

Grebel, Felix, 22, 28
Gruner, Gottlieb Anton, 93n13
GutsMuths, Johann Christoph Friedrich, 89

Hamann, Johann George, 72n9
Hamilton, Alexander, 55
Hancock, John, 52
Helvetic Republic, 62–72, 74–5, 77, 84, 88
Helvetic Revolution, 15, 39 58–60, 84, 112
Herbart, Johann Friedrich, 75
Hirzel, Johann Caspar, 20
historiography, 20, 67, 135, 138–9
Holy Roman Empire, 101–2
How Gertrude Teachers Her Children (Pestalozzi), 70, 74, 77–9
human nature, 59–60
Humboldt, Wilhelm von, 54, 60n1, 80, 87

industrial production, 34
infanticide, 45, 49n7
inner strengthening, 9–10
institutional successes, 74–6
internal conflicts, 98–100
international success, 78–80, 118–19
Iselin, Isaak, 10, 35, 42–3, 52
Ith, Johann Samuel, 74

Jacobi, Friedrich Heinrich, 72n9
Jacobins, 54
Jefferson, Thomas, 8
Jesus Christ, 77–80, 133
Joseph II, 43
July Revolution, 123–4

Kantianism, 89
Kasthofer, Rosette, 111, 122
Kleist, Ewald Christian von, 20
Klopstock, Friedrich Gottlieb, 20
Kohlrausch, Friedrich, 108–9
Krüsi, Hermann, 69, 99, 104, 110–11, 118
Krüsi, Hermann, Jr., 72n11

L'Aspée, Johannes de, 93n12
Lavater, Johann Caspar, 22–3, 30
Leu, Johann Jacob, 18
Leyden, Frederik Auguste van, 87
Lienhard und Gertrud (Pestalozzi), 10, 39–44, 46–8, 51, 65, 79
Louis XIV, 5
Louis XVI, 55
Luther, Martin, 9, 13n12, 23n1, 102–3
Lutheranism, 9, 13n12, 72n9, 140
Luxembourg, 3, 124

Madison, James, 55
Mann, Horace, 126, 131–2, 134–5, 139
Mansfield, Edward Deering, 133–4
Maria Theresa, 43, 112
Marie Antoinette, 55
Marti, Johann Rudolf, 91
Mary II, 11n5
Massachusetts Board of Education, 126
McGuffey, William Holmes, 134–5
McGuffey Readers, 134
Mead, George Herbert, 136
Mediterranean Regional Project (MRP), 141
Meine Lebensschicksale (Pestalozzi), 119–121
Meine Nachforschungen (Pestalozzi), 58–60, 67, 82
Meiners, Christoph, 20
meritocracy, 17, 64, 130
"method," 63, 68–71, 74–82, 82n2, 85–93, 96, 98–104, 106–9, 120, 124, 141
Meyer, Jeremias, 118
Meyer, Johann Rudolf, 46
modernity, 11
modernization, 101, 130–2, 141
modern school, 2–4, 130–2, 135, 137–9, 141–2
monarchy, 16, 44, 51, 54–5, 112, 123
money, politics and, 6–8
Monoe, James, 132
Monroe, Paul, 134–5, 138
Monroe Doctrine, 132

Index

Montesquieu, 20–1, 24n16
moral discourse, 136–9
moral freedom, 40
morality, 56–7
Moral Political and Historical Society, 23, 28–30
Moser, Christoph Ferdinand, 88–9
mothers, 2–3, 49n7, 71, 75, 89, 109, 124,
Müller, Christoph Heinrich, 29–30

Napoleon I, 80, 84, 86–7, 104, 118, 130, 132
Nassau-Usingen, Duke of, 87
natural course, 70
natural law, 44–7, 55–7, 64
Netherlands, 3, 7, 12n11, 87, 124
Neuhof, 32–6, 39, 42, 119–23
Neuhof writings, 35–6
Nicolovius, Georg Heinrich Ludwig, 72n9, 80, 87, 90, 104, 118, 130
Niederer, Johannes, 81, 99–100, 104, 109–11, 118, 121, 123
Norway, 3

Old Swiss Confederation, 20, 25n21, 62, 64
oligarchization, 15, 17, 19–21, 39, 57, 64
Order of the Illuminati, 43
Organization for Economic Cooperation and Development (OECD), 4, 141

parents, 87–90
Parson, Talcott, 130
patriotism, 7, 19, 28, 44
Patterson, William, 6
pedagogy, 3
Pestalozzi, Heinrich Karl, 119
Pestalozzi, Johann Heinrich
  career and family decisions for, 30–3
  charisma of, 95–104, 108
  childhood and youth, 27–30
  collected works, 113
  cult of, 78–80, 123–7
  death of, 122–7
  debate with Tscharner, 34–6
  An die Unschuld, den Ernst und den Edelmut, 111–13
  disillusionment of, 42–4
  educational public and, 90–2
  educational turn and, 1–4, 9, 10, 11
  French Revolution and, 54–5
  Helvetic Republic and, 62–72
  How Gertrude Teachers Her Children, 70, 74, 77, 79
  internationalization of, 118–19
  legacy of, 129–43
  marriage of, 31–3
  Meine Lebensschicksale, 120–1
  Meine Nachforschungen, 58–60
  Neuhof farmhouse, 32–4, 39, 42
  official recognition, fight for, 106–9
  on political order, 50–61
  politics of, 112
  as reformer, 38–49
  Schwanengesang, 120
  in Stans, 66–8
  success for, 73–82, 95–104
  suffering and redemption for, 76–8
  troubled years for, 109–11
  writings of, 39–44, 46–8, 65
  Zurich and, 14–25
Pestalozzian schools, 89, 90–2
Pestalozzi method, 62–72, 74–6, 80–2, 85–93, 96, 98–104, 106–9, 124
Pestalozzi School, 80
Plamann, Johann Ernst, 90, 93n11
Plato, 5
political order, 50–61
political reforms, 39–42
politics, 80–2, 112
  England, 7, 12n10
  money and, 6, 7–8, 12n9
  republican, 11, 16–17, 40
  U.S., 7
  Zurich, 15–17
poor, school for the, 113–15
Preisig, Johannes, 90, 93n10
private banking, 18–19
professionalization, 139
progress, 5–8, 11
propaganda, 74–6

Index

property, 44–46, 51–4, 58–60
Protestantism, 8–11, 15, 18, 23n1, 133–4, 141
Prussia, 80, 86, 87, 101, 104, 106, 130
public education, 3
Puritans, 7

Reading Society of the Lake, 57–8
reason, 6, 10
reception, 135–6
redemption, 76–7, 133–4, 139–42
Reformation in Zurich, 7, 9
Reformed Protestantism, 8–9, 15, 23n1, 80–1
Reign of Terror, 51, 54–5, 56–7
religion, 8–11, 46, 74, 79, 81, 94n13
religion in education, 97, 99–100, 113
Republic (Plato), 5
republican government, 16–17, 40
republican youth movement, 15, 21–3, 27–30
republic of virtue, 33–4, 42, 45–7, 64–6, 111–13
republicanism, 7, 9–10, 15, 17, 27, 33, 39–40, 81, 140
Restoration, 118, 130
Rougemont, Georges de, 91
Rousseau, Jean-Jacques, 2, 23n1, 27, 30–1, 39, 45, 67, 81
rural poor, 35–6, 38–49
Russia, 86

Schiller, Friedrich, 25n17
Schmid, Gertrud Helena, 91
Schmid, Joseph, 109–11, 113–15, 118–23
Schmidt, Johann Marius Friedrich, 90
Schrötter, Friedrich Leopold von, 87
Schulthess, Anna, 31–3, 66, 70
Schulthess, Hans Jacob, 34
Schulthess, Johannes, 30
Schwanengesang (Pestalozzi), 120
Second Great Awakening, 133, 136
Seeley, Levi, 138
sense-impression, 70–1, 75
Shoup, William J., 137–8
Skinner, Quentin, 135, 142

social contract, 45, 56, 59–60
The Social Contract (Rousseau), 30–1
social obligation, 51–4
social problems, educationalization of, 1–13, 54, 71, 88
soul, educational strengthening of, 8–11
Soyaux, Adolf, 78
Soviet Union, 140
Spain, 86–7, 92n3
Stans, 63, 66–9
Stapfer, Philipp Albert, 69–70, 74
state boards of education, 126
Steinmüller, Johann Rudolf, 75
super magistrate, 43
Süvern, Johann Wilhelm von, 87, 130
Sweden, 3
Swiss Reformed Protestantism, 9
Swiss republics, 42–4
Switzerland, 2–3, 8, 15, 18, 23, 23n1, 25n21, 30, 33–5, 39, 55, 57, 63–5, 68–9, 71n5, 72n8, 72n12, 74–5, 80–1, 85–6, 89–91, 93n13, 106–7, 110–11, 116n8, 124, 126
see also Zurich *and* Vaud
Synge, John, 133

teacher education, 2–3, 88, 136–9
Tell, Wilhelm, 21, 72n6
Tiedge, Christoph August, 90
Tillich, Ernst, 89
Tories, 7
Treaty of Tilsit, 101
Tscharner, Johann Baptista von, 85
Tscharner, Niklaus Emanuel von, 35–6
Tschiffeli, Johann Rudolf, 33
Tufts, James Hayden, 136
tulip mania, 7, 12n11

UNESCO, 4
United Nations, 4
United States, 3, 7–8, 55, 132–9
U.S. Constitution, 8, 51
Usteri, Paul, 82

Valltravers, Johann Rodolph de, 51–2

Vaud, 85, 111, 119
Versailles, 18
virtue, 7–8, 10, 33–4, 45–6
vocational education, 44–6, 48, 51, 56, 60, 67–9, 96
Vogel, David, 81
Vögelin, Hans Conrad, 9, 28
Voltaire, 43
von Fellenberg, Philipp Emanuel, 106
von Haller, Karl Ludwig, 118
von Türk, Wilhem Christian, 89–90

Waldmann, Hans, 57
War of the Second Coalition, 72n12
Warren, Mercy Otis, 16, 24n3
Washington, George, 55
Wattenwyl, Niklaus Rudolf von, 84
Weiss, Christian, 89
Whigs, 7, 12n10
Wieland, Christoph Martin, 20, 78
William III, 11n5, 87, 90
Wolfowitz, Paul, 141
World Bank, 4, 141

youth movement, 15, 21–3, 27–30
Yverdon institute, 79–80, 85, 87, 90–2, 96–100, 107–11, 114, 118–20

Zinzendorf, Karl Johann Christian von, 43–4
Zunft zur Meisen, 19
Zurich
   architecture, 19
   commercialization of societal life in, 17–19
   constitution of, 15–16
   corruption and decline in, 19–21
   political organization of eighteenth century, 15–17
   Protestantism in, 7, 8, 9, 14–15, 18
   republican youth movement in, 21–3, 27–30
Zurich Academy, 20–1, 27, 28
Zwingli, Huldrych, 23n1, 41, 57
Zwinglianism, 9, 72n9, 80–1

GPSR Compliance
The European Union's (EU) General Product Safety Regulation (GPSR) is a set of rules that requires consumer products to be safe and our obligations to ensure this.

If you have any concerns about our products, you can contact us on

ProductSafety@springernature.com

In case Publisher is established outside the EU, the EU authorized representative is:

Springer Nature Customer Service Center GmbH
Europaplatz 3
69115 Heidelberg, Germany